I0158909

Quitnic
A NEW DAWN RISING

BRIAN READ

© 2013

QUITNIC: A NEW DAWN RISING *BY BRIAN READ*

ACKNOWLEDGEMENTS

A special word of thanks to my wife Linda and children Mark, Bruce and Alison who spent many stressful years hoping for the day when I would finally quit smoking. Also a word of thanks to those reviewed the book for me; My wife Linda, Wayne Gordon, Sue Rusconi and Marion Tapson. Your inputs are greatly appreciated.

All Bible quotations are either from the "New International Version" (NIV) or the "New King James Version" (NKJV)

Layout: Redcrayon Design

Published by Brian Read, Fourways, South Africa.

Chapters		page
1.	INTRODUCTION	7
2.	UNDERSTANDING ADDICTIONS	12
2.1.	The physical aspect of addiction (chemical dependence)	12
2.2.	The mental aspect of addiction	14
2.3.	The spiritual aspect of addiction	15
2.4.	Causes of addiction	15
2.5.	Cure or no cure	17
3.	UNDERSTANDING STRESS	19
4.	REASONS FOR QUITTING	26
4.1.	Psychological effects	26
	The start	26
	The downward spiral	28
	The lies	29
	The self-deception	30
	After quitting	31
4.2.	Day-to-day living	33
	Planning your activities	33
	Smoking limits your activities	33
	Smoking limits your achievements	33
4.3.	Contents of tobacco smoke	34
4.4.	Potentially fatal diseases	35
4.5.	Smoking and reproduction	38
4.6.	Second-hand or environmental smoke	39
4.7.	Non-fatal diseases	40
5.	PHYSICAL ASPECTS OF ADDICTION	41
5.1.	A word of caution	41
5.2.	Different medications	41
	Varenicline (Champix or Chantix)	42
	Bupropion (Zyban or Wellbutrin)	42
	Nicotine Replacement Therapy (NRT)	43
6.	MENTAL AND EMOTIONAL ASPECTS OF ADDICTION	44
6.1.	Commitment	45
	Removing the fear of quitting	47
6.2.	The alternative to fear	52
7.	DEVISING A QUIT PROGRAMME	55
7.1.	Quit date	55
7.2.	Tell family and friends	55
7.3.	Planning a quitting programme	56
	Review the methods described in this book	56
	Find out more about medication	57
	Support services	57

Quitnic

		page
8.	PREPARATION PHASE	59
8.1.	Journal/diary	59
8.2.	List how you feel and why you want to quit	59
8.3.	List the benefits of quitting	62
8.4.	Describe your new dawn rising	65
8.5.	Setting new values	67
	Family values	68
	Work values	69
8.6.	New lifestyle	71
	Healthy lifestyle	72
	Hobbies	72
8.7.	Prepare strategies for your first few days	72
8.8.	Identify triggers	74
9.	STARTING OUT	77
9.1.	The night before	77
9.2.	The first few days	77
Dealing with common hurdles		77
Dealing with anger		79
10.	STAYING QUIT	81
11.	EXERCISE	87
12.	RELAPSES	91
13.	ALLEN CARR	93
14.	NICOTINE ANONYMOUS (NICA)	96
14.1.	Introduction	96
14.2.	Twelve Steps of Nicotine Anonymous	101
NicA Step 1		102
NicA Step 2		102
NicA Step 3		102
NicA Step 4		103
NicA Step 5		103
NicA Step 6		103
NicA Step 7		104
NicA Step 8		105
NicA Step 9		105
NicA Step 10		106
NicA Step 11		106
NicA Step 12		106
15.	CHRISTIAN LIFESTYLE APPROACH – THE TRUTH WILL SET YOU FREE	109
15.1.	Getting started	114
15.2.	Submission to God's will	115
15.3.	A new life in Christ	115
15.4.	Healing and growth	116
Getting to know Jesus		117
Getting to know yourself		118
Conclusion		119
Bibliography		120

Quitnic ————————————————————————————————————

CHAPTER 1 - INTRODUCTION

You are probably not ready to quit smoking.

You are probably fearful of what lies ahead.

You are not being asked to quit smoking. All you are being asked to do is to read this book and devise a quit programme.

You do not need to quit just yet. All you need to do at this stage is read this book and follow the suggestions. When you are ready it will be time to quit.

This book will take you through a process that will clear away your fears, to a point at which you will experience a keen sense of excitement, anticipation and apprehension and will be keen to give it a go. If you follow the process diligently you will reach the stage at which your mind is clear on what you want to achieve and how to get there.

As you read this book I want you to focus on the miracle of a new dawn rising and make it your own. Start thinking of a fresh, healthy new start as you put the smothering filth of smoke behind you. I want to promise you that achieving this can be much easier than most people think. You need to attack quitting from both the negative and positive aspects. It can be rather difficult to simply have to quit; it is much easier to motivate yourself to take up an exciting new lifestyle that precludes or discourages smoking. Then, if you can combine both the negative and the positive aspects, you will have a very powerful tool. Add to that some help from the medical profession and it is even easier.

One of the most important keys to success is replacing your old lifestyle with a new lifestyle.

I have personally battled nicotine addiction for more than fifty years of my life. I have given up many times, for periods ranging from six years to a few weeks or even a day or two. I have researched the findings of scientists and counsellors who deal with the problem of addictions. I have also drawn on the experiences of many others who, like you and I, have fought the battle personally. I have currently been free of nicotine for over 20 months and have never felt more positive about the future than now.

My promise that quitting can be much easier than most people think is not a hollow one. You can look forward to a new dawn rising as you cleanse yourself of the burden that nicotine has placed on you.

This book will show you that quitting is easy, provided you work hard at it. The good news is that it is just hard work - nothing to fear, nothing to get stressed about.

Quitting is a process. By reading this book you are making a start. You may need to be patient, as it could take some time before you are ready to quit. The important thing is that you have started on a journey. All you need to do now is to keep walking: one step at a time and you will get there.

One of your first steps will be to start making your own notes as you go. You can highlight sentences in the book and make notes in the margin, or even keep a separate note book. You will need these notes to help you develop your own tailor-made quitting programme. You will also need to think about what you are reading and add your own ideas and observations. As mentioned above, it requires some work on your behalf.

Depending on where you obtain your statistics, the average smoker will die between 7 and 20 years before the average non-smoker. Tobacco is believed to be the single biggest cause of preventable death worldwide. Statistics show that ⅓ to ½ smokers of all will die as a direct result of their smoking. This can be from diseases such as cancer, cardiovascular disease or emphysema, often only after years of suffering. We all think that we will give up in time and get away with it, but mostly we do not. I have suffered a heart attack and, because of my smoking, my chances of having another one are higher than they would have been if I had never smoked. I have chronic bronchitis and my lung capacity is permanently compromised, all as a direct result of smoking. Please don't leave it too late. Those who do, like millions before them, have to face their loved ones and tell them that they are dying from self-inflicted illness.

Sorry about that bad news, but it is important to get it up front if we are to get what we are dealing with in perspective right from the start. We are dealing with a killer, and we must deal with it boldly.

Many books on quitting smoking will present you with a specific formula for quitting. This one is different. I have tried to make my approach as holistic as possible and to present you with as many different techniques that made sense to me as I could find. Like all addictions, there are three aspects of a nicotine addiction: physical, mental and spiritual (PMS). (Some people divide the mental into mental and emotional.) Much of the literature only deals with one or two of these aspects. The good news is that there are a number of different tried and tested ways of dealing with each one of these aspects. What I propose you do is to study the different techniques presented in this book and then make up your own combination of techniques that suits you. I would recommend that you choose at least one approach to deal with each of these aspects. Research has shown that using a combination of just two appropriate techniques can more than double your chance of success. This, together with some powerful new weapons that recent research has provided, should greatly enhance your chances of quitting successfully. To this you can add the positive aspect of developing a whole new lifestyle.

There are many horror stories about how difficult it is to quit smoking and about the dreadful withdrawal symptoms, but remember that these are an accumulation of the worst-case scenarios, and are often cases in which none of the modern medications or techniques were used. What is more, many who have tried and failed like to exaggerate in order to justify their failure and to create a good story. In reality, millions of ex-smokers worldwide will tell you that their personal experience, once they knew how and once they were committed, wasn't that difficult at all. A lot depends on your attitude. As you read this book, try and develop a positive attitude.

Every smoker is different and no one technique suits all, so this book will present you with a wide range of techniques from which to choose. The aim is to equip you with the necessary knowledge, skills, tools, courage, motivation and mind-set to quit smoking and to remain free. What you are going to do is study this book and develop an approach and programme, and then you should be well on your way to a fresh new start.

Fear is possibly one of the greatest stumbling blocks for people wanting to quit. The statistics, in one study, show that almost 70% of respondents failed even to attempt to quit due to fear. Fear can take a number of forms: it can be fear of failure or fear of the anticipated stress that a quit attempt is likely to cause, amongst others. Hopefully, by the time you have finished this book your fear will be greatly diminished. This fear should be replaced by some mixed emotions of excitement, apprehension and anticipation. This is similar to what you might experience when embarking on some challenging adventure.

There will be hurdles along the way; however, none of these will be hurdles that other smokers before you have not faced. I have obtained testimony from other smokers and together with other literature on the subject I believe it will be possible to help you to anticipate most of the hurdles you are likely to encounter. It will also be possible to provide some guidance as to how these hurdles can be overcome.

Research has shown that approximately half of all quit attempts are initiated on the spur of the moment. It is believed that you reach a point at which your emotions balancing the pros and cons of quitting are in a state of high tension. At some point you may reach a situation where the discomfort and the sense of urgency becomes greater than the perceived benefits and/or the anticipated difficulties of quitting. Some small event triggers a switch so that all of a sudden the balance swings in favour of quitting. You then generally quit immediately, and about half of such quit attempts are successful. As quit attempts go, this is a very high success rate. The first time I quit was one of these events and I remained free for some six years. This book is designed to lead you to a trigger point at which you will be equipped, ready and enthusiastic about getting on with your quitting exercise.

You will have developed a glorious picture of the exciting future that awaits you – a whole new lifestyle free from slavery to nicotine. You will become fully committed. When your heart is steadfastly set on success, you will have won a major and crucial part of the battle. It will be time to awaken to your new dawn.

You will find a lot of repetition in this book; that is because this is a teaching book. It is designed to teach you how to quit, and you will find that from time to time you will be required to set aside some time to start developing your own quit programme.

Consider quitting as a challenging adventure.

Focus on the miracle of a clean and fresh new dawn rising and make it your own.

Replacing your old lifestyle with a new lifestyle is one of the most important keys to success.

Quitting simply takes hard work – nothing to fear, nothing to get stressed about.

Rid yourself of the burden nicotine has placed on you.

Remember: you are dealing with a killer, and you must deal with it responsibly.

You need three programmes, the physical, mental and spiritual (PMS).

You need to develop a positive attitude.

The aim is to equip you with the necessary knowledge, skills, tools, courage, motivation and mind-set to quit smoking and remain free.

You will learn to look forward to quitting with mixed emotions of excitement, apprehension and anticipation.

You will plan a whole new life free from the slavery to nicotine.

You have started on a journey. Keep walking.

CHAPTER 2 - UNDERSTANDING ADDICTIONS

All addictions are very similar and much of the research is focused on addictions as a whole rather than to specific drugs. Addictive behaviours cover a wide range of substances and activities, including nicotine, alcohol, heroin, gambling, overeating and pornography.

The title of this chapter is misleading, because no one fully understands addictions. Although a number of different models have been proposed, many aspects remain unproven and poorly understood. In many ways, the manner in which addictions work remains a mystery.
Despite the fact that we do not fully understand how addictions work, the different models provide us with much useful information that can help in understanding how to overcome addictions.

The drug found in tobacco, nicotine, is considered to be as addictive as cocaine or heroin. Smoking is a very effective drug-delivery system. It enables the smoker to control the rate at which the drug is delivered, even from low tar cigarettes. The smoke is delivered deep into the smoker's lungs, where nicotine is quickly absorbed into the blood-stream. The blood then carries the nicotine to all parts of the body. Smoking delivers nicotine to the brain even more quickly than drugs injected into a vein. However, after quitting smoking, residual nicotine only remains in the body for approximately four days.
As mentioned in the introduction, there are three aspects to nicotine addiction, physical, mental and spiritual (PMS). I will deal with each separately. I would recommend that you include a strategy for dealing with each one in your programme.

2.1.   The physical aspect of addiction (chemical dependence)
When you smoke you develop a physical/chemical dependence on nicotine. After a while your body develops a certain level of tolerance to the drug. This leads to an increase in the amount smoked in order to get the same effect. In time this stabilises.

As soon as you put out a cigarette, the nicotine level in your body starts to drop. Withdrawal symptoms set in. These include feelings such as restlessness, irritability or anxiety. This is what Allen Carr calls "that empty insecure feeling." The result is that you tolerate this for a while, and then you light another cigarette in order to take away the withdrawal symptoms. This cycle carries on until one day when you finally quit. All you are actually doing by smoking is temporarily allaying the withdrawal symptoms while you add nicotine to your system, thereby ensuring that the symptoms will return.

Physical withdrawal symptoms can take different forms and differ in intensity. Many people do not experience any noticeable physical withdrawal symptoms, whereas others do. Symptoms last from a few days to three weeks. I have personally given up a number of times and have never suffered from any really noticeable physical withdrawal symptoms.

Most smokers have quit numerous times with varying degrees of success depending on the method used in quitting. It is not uncommon for someone to experience significant withdrawal symptoms with one quitting technique and negligible symptoms with another. However, everyone's smoking and quitting experiences are different. What works for one person may not work for another.

It is also common to find that the anticipation of the quitting experience was much worse than it in fact turned out to be.

There is some debate around withdrawal symptoms, making it difficult to get accurate information. Symptoms are rarely separated out into physical and emotional symptoms, which is possibly a reflection of the fact that it is difficult to identify symptoms with certainty. Reporting of symptoms is subjective, and this can lead to them being confused with symptoms from other causes. Furthermore, physical and mental withdrawal symptoms can be confused, making it difficult to know how long to continue with medication. Many ex-smokers believe that the physical withdrawal symptoms are so slight as to be imperceptible. Some people have reported that they have not suffered from any physical withdrawal symptoms.

Although it is very rare, possibly the most significant reported withdrawal symptom is depression. In the unlikely event that you do find you are suffering from depression, you should seek medical help. Commonly reported symptoms include irritability, anxiety, difficulty concentrating, insomnia, restlessness and increased appetite (weight gain). Other symptoms include dizziness, headaches, tiredness, constipation, coughing, sore throat and related complaints, and feelings of frustration, impatience and anger. There are many ways of dealing with these symptoms, even medicinally, if necessary.

I believe that with the techniques this book teaches, you can get the physical withdrawal phase down to an intensity and period of time which will be of negligible concern. Furthermore, this physical side of addiction can be easily and effectively taken care of by medication. There are a number of medication options, which will be dealt with elsewhere in this book.

> **Smoking temporarily allays withdrawal symptoms while you add nicotine to your system, ensuring that the symptoms return.**
>
> **You should be able to get the physical withdrawal phase down to an intensity and period of time that will be of negligible concern.**
>
> **Many people have found that the anticipation of the quitting experience was much worse than it in fact turned out to be.**

2.2. The mental aspect of addiction

Addiction as a whole however involves much more than just the physical addiction that causes withdrawal symptoms. Someone who has quit for a few months, or even years, and who has clearly gotten over the physical aspect of addiction, can easily fall prey again. A number of mechanisms have been proposed that help to explain how someone becomes addicted and can remain addicted even long after a successful quit episode.

One possible mechanism is the development of a powerful habit. Smoking establishes a neurological reward pathway in the brain. Initially, this pathway is fairly weak, but the longer you continue to smoke the stronger it gets. Every time you smoke, more and more positive associations are added to this reward cycle, gradually making it stronger and stronger. When you think about smoking you may be visualising a pack of cigarettes or a particular social occasion in which you are smoking, or perhaps smoking and drinking coffee. Each of these rewarding images gets added to your reward pathway. When you smoke, it is the direct pleasure that you get from smoking that helps to build this reward pathway. Even the withdrawal symptoms add a form of negative reinforcement to the pathway due to the relief you get when you light another cigarette. The pathway starts out as a narrow little track and ends up as what Anthony Robbins (well-known self-help author and motivational speaker) describes as a "neural super-highway." Little wonder you cannot get off this pathway, because all along the way there are hundreds of signs reminding you about smoking and the pleasure and relief it brings. You ignore the negative aspects that lurk on the side like vicious beasts waiting to devour you. They can wait, because as long as your attention remains on the road, they will get you in the end.

Soon we will be looking at some of the negative effects of smoking, and this will start to break down this reward pathway.

It is thought that if the nicotine levels in this pathway drop below a certain level the activity in this pathway drops correspondingly. This creates a kind of "nicotine hunger" or craving, which is only alleviated by smoking another cigarette.

Another possible mechanism operates on the smoker's reaction to the withdrawal symptoms they experience between cigarettes. The feelings of restlessness, irritability or anxiety are relieved as soon as the smoker lights up. With time, the smoker comes mistakenly to believe that smoking really helps in such circumstances. Even though this is not the case, the smoker's own experience leads them to believe that smoking really helps them. This is one of the reasons smokers who have quit even for a substantial period of time sometimes relapse during stressful times in their lives.

Smoking establishes a neurological reward pathway in the brain that you will need to break.

Shortly, we will start to work on breaking down this pathway.

2.3. The spiritual aspect of addiction

Organisations such as Alcoholics Anonymous (AA), Nicotine Anonymous (NicA), the Cancer Association of South Africa (CANSA) and Christian addiction programmes recognise the spiritual side of addictions. In fact AA, NicA and Christian organisations define their quit programmes as spiritual programmes of recovery. The AA and NicA twelve-step programmes consider spiritual principles to be essential elements for recovering from addiction. The success of these programmes is known around the world.

Rather than discuss the spiritual aspect of addiction here, I will leave that to the last two chapters, where NicA and Christian programmes are discussed.

2.4.   Causes of addiction

The causes of addiction are complex and can be different for every smoker. Environmental factors play a major role. These can include things like parents, peers and role models who smoke. A teenager's sense of adventure often leads down a path to smoking. Advertising remains an important factor encouraging people to smoke even today.

It is interesting to listen to people's first experiences with smoking. One soon realises that there are vast differences between people's early experiments. Many people will tell you that they were so disgusted with their first cigarette that they vowed never to try it again. They may tell you how it nearly made them physically ill. There are others who found it unpleasant but became conditioned after a few tries and then, before they knew it, they were addicted. Then there is a third group, into which I fitted. I enjoyed smoking from the very first puff and in those early days never experienced any negative side effects.

We often hear people say that they have an addictive personality. Is it really possible for someone to inherit a genetic makeup that makes them susceptible to addiction? The simple answer is yes, but that is where the simplicity ends.

Genetic studies investigating the possible inheritance of addictive tendencies are very complex. For a start, it seems that a number of different genes could be involved. In fact, it has been concluded that genetic susceptibility to addictions is probably the result of a number of interacting genes.

It is also possible that one set of genes may lead to susceptibility in one person while a different set of genes may be responsible in another person. A set of genes that cause a person to become addicted to nicotine will probably not cause them to become addicted to alcohol. However, there appear to be a number of linkages and most alcoholics are also addicted to nicotine. Nicotine addicts can also be susceptible to alcohol addiction, but to a much lesser extent. Genetic studies are also strongly influenced by environmental factors. For example, a person both of whose parents are heavy smokers is also likely to smoke. This could be due to a genetic link, purely to environmental factors, or to a combination of both influences. Despite the complexity involved in trying to sort this one out, scientists have concluded that some people are genetically more prone to becoming addicted than others.

Some people have inherited genetic factors that make them biologically more likely to become addicts. However, they first have to start taking the drug in order to become addicted. Their genetic makeup will not lead them to the drug in the first place but will only affect them once they have tried the drug.

This predisposition is strongly influenced by environmental factors. In the absence of outside influences, someone who is genetically more likely to become a smoker may never try smoking and may remain unaffected for their entire life.

Addiction can be due to environmental factors alone or a combination of genetic and environmental factors. However, addiction cannot be due to genetic factors alone. Genetic factors will not cause you to become addicted unless there is some environmental factor that leads you to take the drug in the first place.

No two people's addiction is the same, which is why this book offers you a range of different treatments to select from. A treatment that works for someone else may not work for you.

Either environmental factors, or genetic factors, or some combination of both can lead to addiction.

Addiction cannot be due to genetic factors alone.

2.5.   Cure or no cure

This is a controversial question, with widely differing opinions held by various people.

Nicotine Anonymous makes it very clear that attaining abstinence from nicotine can be a healing, but there is no absolute cure. They see remaining free as an on-going journey that you take one day at a time. Relapses are all too common with nicotine addiction. This is why Nicotine Anonymous suggests that members continue attending meetings for the rest of their lives. They also find that long-term encouragement in helping others is a spiritual expression of their gratitude for the freedom they have received, and that this helps them to stay free. They could hardly be as helpful to others if they themselves had relapsed.

Others believe that certain methods do offer a cure. This may partly depend on your definition of a cure. It is very difficult to tell whether a person is cured or not. If someone has not smoked for 10 years, would you consider that person cured? I know from personal experience that even after 6 years it was very easy to fall back into the trap. My father quit when he was 55 and never smoked again in the remaining 43 years of his life. However, that does not prove that he was cured: I remember him telling me many years after he quit that he still had occasional cravings. One thing I am sure of, however, is that the craving drops exponentially, and in a very short time it can be virtually non-existent. I also believe that if you focus on building a new and healthier lifestyle, you will soon forget about the time when you used to be a smoker. I currently feel as though I am cured, but I still very occasionally have a very short-lived desire for a cigarette. I have finally learned the lesson that I can never ever have another puff without it almost certainly turning me into a smoker once more.

Every book on quitting will tell you that you can never risk having another puff. I am sure you believe this. However, there is a difference between believing and knowing. I believe that the world orbits around the sun along an elliptical path. However, I am open to correction on this issue. On the other hand, I know that if I put my hand into a flame I will get burned. I know this because I have been burned in this way a number of times. I have quit on a number of occasions and always believed that if I ever had another puff I could easily relapse. I needed to go through the quitting process and then relapse several times before I came to know for absolute certain that if I ever have another puff I will relapse once again. This is one of the hardest lessons to internalise and make your own.

> **Nicotine Anonymous makes it very clear that attaining abstinence from nicotine can be a healing, but there is no absolute cure.**
>
> **Other people believe that certain methods do offer a cure.**

CHAPTER 3 - UNDERSTANDING STRESS

It is important to understand the role stress plays in the lives of smokers. It is widely believed that smoking relieves stress, but this not strictly true. Smoking appears to cause stress and the stress it causes can be very harmful to your health and wellbeing. Some studies have found that smokers suffer higher levels of everyday stress than non-smokers. How can this be? In order to answer this question clearly it is necessary to understand a bit more about how stress operates and how it affects our bodies.

We all suffer stress in our lives, and it is in fact a significant problem in the modern western world. Many illnesses are in some way or another influenced by stress.

As already mentioned, it appears that smoking only relieves the stress that it caused in the first place. There are however many things that cause stress in your life. If you remove smoking as a cause of stress, you are left with the remaining causes. It will be helpful if you can identify the other factors causing stress in your life and then deal with them separately.

Most smokers have quit a number of times and then at some stage they have relapsed. They often report that stress was the main factor leading them back into the trap. This is the reality, despite the fact that smoking does not relieve any pre-existing stress but simply raises a person's overall level of stress.

Stress plays an important role in human biology, and it is not always bad. Imagine you are walking down a path and suddenly you come across a cobra with its head raised and ready to strike. Such an encounter will raise your stress levels through the roof before you have time to think. What happens next is probably a blur in most people's minds because it all happens so quickly. In fact, the biological processes that take place and the speed with which they occur are almost miraculous. Endocrine glands in your body release hormones, particularly adrenaline and cortisol, into your blood stream. This causes your heart rate to increase, your blood pressure to rise, your muscles to tighten, your breath to quicken and your senses to heighten all in a split second. This prepares you for the next step, commonly referred to as the "fight or flight" response. Whatever way you decide to react to the problem, it is probably all over in an amazingly short time, and hopefully in a manner that allows you to escape safely. The stress response has clearly saved countless people's lives in such situations. Stress can also help to motivate you to perform under pressure, such as during a business presentation. On the other side of the coin, however, stress can cause an awful amount of damage.

Such damaging stress is that caused by certain on-going situations such as strained family relationships, stress in the work place or an inability to forgive someone for a wrong perpetrated against you. These stress factors can affect you on a daily basis. We all know that this type of stress can hang over us like a cloud for extended periods of time. This type of stress is referred to as chronic stress, and includes the stress caused by smoking. Unfortunately, our biological systems deal with all types of stress in much the same way: by releasing adrenalin and cortisol.

The adrenalin causes your heart to beat faster and more strongly in order to provide you with the strength and speed to escape from a life-threatening situation. The adrenalin also expands the blood vessels to increase the flow of blood to the brain and muscles. At the same time, it constricts the blood vessels feeding certain other organs that are less important to the "fight or flight" response.

Cortisol does a number of things. Of most significance to our discussion is the fact that cortisol helps your body to provide the extra energy needed to respond appropriately to any stressful situation. To do this it temporarily slows down certain systems and bodily functions that are less important in a "fight or flight" situation. Now comes the crunch: one of the systems that is suppressed in this way is the immune system. It is easy to imagine what on-going, or chronic, stress due to smoking does to your immune system in the long run. This makes it more difficult for your body to fight off disease.

Stress is believed to affect your health in other ways in addition to your immune system. Stress is believed to play a more direct role in cardiovascular diseases such as heart attacks and strokes. This makes it a double whammy, because smoking already makes you prone to so many diseases, including cardiovascular diseases, lung problems and various forms of cancer. Now, thanks to the stress caused by smoking, you are less capable of fighting off the many illnesses that come your way. This further saps your energy, both physical and mental, often making your life quite miserable.

In addition to the above, there is another way in which stress is thought to contribute to poor health. People who are stressed often behave in ways which further impede good health. For one, they tend to exercise less than less stressed people, and it is well known that exercise reduces stress levels. They also often have poor eating habits, often don't sleep well, tend to smoke more and do not comply with medical treatment regimes. Smokers are thought to be particularly prone to the last one. I would always resist visiting the doctor because I was concerned that he would tell me that the only thing wrong with me was my smoking and that he had no medication that could help that. That was news that I dreaded having to tell my family.

The important questions we want answered is, how will stress affect our quitting attempt and how can we deal with this aspect of the programme? Although this book is not about managing stress, there are a few things worth mentioning here. There is a lot of useful literature available, and it is worth getting a professional to advise you in this regard. A doctor may even be able to prescribe medication.
It is important to recognise that there are usually a number of things that may cause stress in our lives. If we are going to quit, we will only be removing one of those causes. A problem you are likely to face, especially in the first few days after you have quit, is considerably heightened stress levels as you battle the craving for nicotine and the habit that has been a part of your life for so long. As you prepare for your quit day it is worth considering how you will deal with this aspect. Fortunately, there are many methods available to you.

Possibly one of the first ways you should consider is medication to help you quit, whether it be prescription medicines or nicotine replacement therapy such as nicotine gums. These are all dealt with in more detail later in this book. Medications are generally considered to be an important part of any quit programme. They are widely reported to enhance your chances of quitting successfully significantly. Medications all deal with the physical side of the addiction, which is also referred to as the acute phase (i.e. the P of PMS). This phase generally only lasts for a few days, although in some cases it can persist for longer. Most quit programmes strongly recommend that you use some form of medication to help you quit.

It is well worth considering all the other stress factors in your life. You could do some soul-searching and try and identify the things that cause you stress on a day-to-day basis. Consider each one in turn and ask yourself what you can do about it. Make a list of all the things that cause you stress. If you put your mind to it, there are bound to be areas of stress in your life that can be reduced. Some typical things other than smoking that cause many of us daily stress include the following:

• Interpersonal relationships (family, friends, work colleagues);
• Feeling overwhelmed and unable to cope with the situation at work or in the home;
• An unbalanced lifestyle;
• Anger;
• Embarrassing mistakes of the past – put the past behind you as you look forward to your new dawn; and
• Un-forgiveness is one of the biggest and most destructive stressors in our present day society.

Un-forgiveness probably requires some further explanation. Most of us have been angered by past events in our life and may find it difficult to forgive the person who caused this anger. Such anger can continue to cause chronic stress in our lives until such time as we are able to forgive the person who caused our anger in the first place. There are times when you may consider it to be impossible to forgive. Many people believe that they will be able to find closure if justice is done. Unfortunately, it does not work that way. Forgiveness is the only cure. Forgiveness is not about letting the person who angered you off the hook, it is about releasing yourself from the destructive stress the anger is causing you, it is about bringing peace into your life.

In addition to things that cause stress in your life there are also things that determine how you react to stressful situations:

• If you have a good support network, with strong ties to family and friends, this can act as an effective buffer against stressful times and situations. Call on family and friends for support.
• If you lack self-confidence, this can cause you to experience stressful

situations more intensely than someone who is self-confident.

• Your outlook and attitude can affect how you react to stressful situations. For example road-rage may be an example of someone with a bad attitude.

• Pessimists can expect to lead far more stressful lives than optimists.

There are many things that can be done to relieve stress, a few of which are discussed briefly below.

To manage stress you may be able to change the stressful situation in a way that reduces your stress levels. Alternatively, you can change the way you react to this stressful situation. In other situations you can make time for rest and relaxation.

You should carefully consider your lifestyle. Do you have a balanced lifestyle? If not, consider what you can do to change it.

One of the best methods for someone who is struggling with the stress of craving a cigarette is deep breathing. Take a few moments off from what you are doing and relax. It is a good idea to close your eyes, take a gentle deep breath and breathe out slowly, making a conscious effort to relax as you do so. Do this a few times; it is amazing how effective it is. Not only does it help you to relax and shed some of your stress, but it also focuses your mind on something else. It is therefore very likely that by the time you have finished your deep breathing exercise your craving will also have dissipated.

Another thing you can do is to quieten your mind. Say a brief prayer. Write down as many motivational thoughts regarding your quit programme as you can. Keep them on cards in your pocket (or some other convenient place) and refer to them regularly.

Take a break from what you are doing: take a walk down the corridor and go and get a cup of tea. However, if tea-time was one of those times when you would normally have a cigarette, this may not be a good idea. Avoid things that remind you of smoking as they act as triggers to set off your craving.

If you are feeling stressed at work it may be an idea to speak to your boss about ways of reducing this stress. Maybe you need to say no to some of the tasks that come your way. You may be able to rearrange your work or responsibilities to make them more manageable.

If you find yourself becoming angered regularly it may be a good idea to see if you can enrol for an anger management course, or read a good book on the subject. Another helpful tactic is to try and put yourself into the shoes of the person who has angered you. Similarly, if you are suffering from un-forgiveness, try putting yourself in the shoes of the person whom you find it difficult to forgive. Try and understand why they did what it was that angered you. Even people who have been raped or who have had a loved one murdered have found it in their hearts to forgive. Forgiveness is not about letting the perpetrator off the hook, it is about letting yourself off the hook. If you can forgive, you can save yourself an awful lot of stress and suffering. Once again, there are counsellors who can help as well as a number of good books on the subject.

Regular exercise is well known as a means to manage stress levels. Most quit programmes recommend that you take up some form of exercise. This is doubly helpful, because not only does it help to manage your stress levels, but it also gives you a new and healthier goal to focus on. One of the most highly recommended forms of exercise in quit programmes is walking. It is not necessary to undertake any form of intense training as you would, for example, for athletics. All you need is some form of aerobic exercise that raises your heart rate, improves your health and cardiovascular performance and helps you control your weight. It is sometimes recommended that you raise your heart rate to approximately 75% of (220 beats per minute, minus your age). Another approximation is 180 beats per minute, minus your age. You should probably strive to exercise for 30 to 40 minutes at least three or four days a week. If you cannot manage this, any exercise is better than nothing.

When you first started this chapter, there is a good chance that you believed that smoking reduces stress. In future, every time you light up I want you to think about exactly what it is that smoking is doing for you, from the positive and negative perspectives. I want you to recognise that every time you smoke you are prolonging the time you have to suffer nicotine-induced stress.

Smoking only relieves the stress that it caused in the first place.

Our bodies deal with all types of stress in much the same way: by releasing adrenalin and cortisol.

A side effect of this is that your immune system is suppressed.

In the first few days after you have quit, your stress levels could very likely be considerably heightened.

As you prepare for your quit day it is worth considering how you will deal with stress.

Write down as many motivational thoughts as you can and keep them on cards in your pocket.

Deep breathing can help you relax and overcome stress.

Get regular exercise.

CHAPTER 4 - REASONS FOR QUITTING

If you are going to conquer the devil you hate, you have to get him out in the open and vulnerable. You need a good understanding of all the angles from which he is likely to attack. The more aware you are of the ways in which smoking adversely affects absolutely every aspect of your life, the more powerfully you will want to quit. The more powerfully you want to quit, the easier it will be. And together with the other techniques this book will teach you, it will be easier still.

As smokers, many of us tend to hide from the truth about our smoking. When the doctor asks how many cigarettes we smoke, many of us tend to reduce the number by 20% to 30%, which is probably just as well, because he probably adds 20% to 30% to the number we give him. Nicotine Anonymous teaches its members that it is time to be honest. It is time to put away all those rationalisations that we have used as excuses for not quitting. We need to be honest with ourselves and with those near and dear to us.

In recent years my health problems have been almost entirely related to smoking. Since I had a heart attack some eight years ago, I have probably spent more than US$200 a month on what would otherwise have been unnecessary medical expenses. I now have a number of chronic conditions that are going to be with me for the rest of my life. Some of these are due to previous unwise life choices. Although I have stopped smoking, those increased medical expenses remain. I am hoping that they will decrease over the next few years. However, that is most probably a vain hope: the damage has been done. I have reached that time of my life when old age is setting in and I can probably expect my medical expenses to increase. I am trying to eat more wisely, control my stress levels and get more exercise. This requires a lot of discipline and I am not doing nearly as well as I would like to in this regard. The best opportunity I had to turn my health around is way behind me. It's time to pick up the results.

This next section is the bad news section of this book. It is essential that you read this if you are to appreciate the good news to follow and if you are to find the motivation necessary to empower you.

The more powerfully you want to quit, the easier it will be.

Writing out a list of reasons why you want to quit will take you a significant way along the path. Keep walking.

Writing these lists and referring to them regularly will increase the power of your desire to quit.

You can put some of the main points onto cards, which you can place in your pocket and refer to regularly.

4.1. Psychological effects
Smokers generally face an on-going psychological battle that causes much stress and reduces the potential level of happiness in their lives. There are constant reminders at the back of their minds of all the horrors of smoking and the harm that they are causing themselves and their loved ones. However, there is a way of coping with this.

When people find themselves having to face up to things like the scary consequences of their actions, they tend to put these things partly out of their conscious minds. They have heard about all the negative consequences of smoking frequently. However, they avoid investigating these in any detail because they fear finding out exactly what it is they will ultimately have to face up to.

It is time for you to start to reflect on all the ways in which smoking affects your mental wellbeing. Start keeping some notes, even if they are scribbled in the margins of this book. This section is based on the experiences of dozens of smokers, so you should find quite a lot in common with your own experience.

The start
Different people experience nicotine addiction differently: its hold on one person is not the same as its hold on the next. When people first start smoking they commonly only experience the positive side. The emotions experienced with this phase include things such as: manliness, adult, in control, independent, profound, macho, and sophisticated.

The downward spiral

The longer you continue smoking and the more you smoke, so the negative effects accumulate. Unfortunately, they accumulate so slowly as to be almost imperceptible and at first everything seems normal. As time goes by, so you tend to become more aware of all these negative effects. However, most smokers tend to put these out of their minds. The result is that the problem has to get a lot worse before you react to it.

Eventually the penny starts to drop and you begin to become more aware of what is happening to you. You start to realise that smoking rules your life in so many ways.

For many smokers, the first thing they think about when they get up in the morning is having a smoke. Even if it causes them to cough violently, they just have to have it. Often they wake up still feeling tired, maybe anxious and lacking energy and enthusiasm for the day ahead. The solution is another cigarette. The temporary relief it brings only serves to increase the problem in the longer term.

Social pressures start to bear on you. Smoking is looked down on by so many people these days. When you enter the smoking section of a restaurant you can feel the eyes of everyone looking at you and thinking "poor sucker." You feel guilty for the non-smoker who you have dragged in to that section of the establishment. You feel ashamed. Your desperate need to smoke is too strong to be outweighed by your sense of guilt and shame. When you have to get up from your desk at work and go off for a quiet smoke you begin to feel the shame of your actions. You hope people don't notice how often you disappear. You become stressed because you cannot go as often as you would like. You feel trapped, there seems to be nothing you can do about it. You are a slave to nicotine.

Nicotine becomes a part of your every waking hour. As your health deteriorates so your sense of guilt towards yourself and your loved ones grows. Your emotions may become a mixture of self-loathing, shame, anger, longing and despair.

You begin to realise that nicotine is slowly gaining more and more control of your life. However, you remain convinced that you will stop before it's too late. You are likely to experience a growing sense of shame and fear.

You dread the day when you will eventually have to quit, but are thankful that, at least at this stage, you can put it off until a later date.

In the back of your mind you may recognise that your behaviour is that of a depraved addict, insanely pursuing nicotine as it progressively robs you of your quality of life. You have probably all experienced those awful moments when you realise you are out of cigarettes and there are none to be had. So many of us have been so desperate that we have bummed off strangers, lifted cigarette butts out of ashtrays, sifted through the rubbish bin, searched the empty packet for a second and third time, climbed into the car late at night in mid-winter and driven miles to the nearest all-night store.

The great majority of smokers reading this will probably have tried to quit more than once before, and quite possibly there will be a history of many failed attempts. Some of those attempts may not even have really gotten underway before they were curtailed within a few hours of starting. Many may only have lasted for a day or two. As the number of failed attempts mounts so you may start to become fearful as you begin to realise just how strong a hold nicotine has on you. As the number of futile attempts grows, you may start to become desperate, and your self-esteem may start to decline.

Smokers often tend to start becoming increasingly ashamed as they continue to smoke while others manage to quit. Smokers often feel guilty, and all this causes their stress levels to increase. They may start to feel disgusted with themselves, weak, worthless, incompetent, hopeless, angry and fearful of the potential consequences. They start to feel that they are on a downward spiral towards an early and possibly painful death.

Remember that what you have read above is based on the experiences of many ex-smokers who escaped the trap, which means that you can also escape.

The lies
In his book Easy Way to Stop Smoking, Allen Carr writes, "All smokers are liars. I don't mean that they are basically dishonest people. In all other respects they might be honest, but about their smoking they lie. It's not their fault; they have to and the worst part is that they lie to themselves."

When I first read this I thought Carr was being a bit harsh. What he said was certainly true of me, but all smokers? I doubted it. However, the more I have read about the subject, and especially other smoker's testimonies, the more I have come to realise that he is probably very close to the mark.

If you started smoking when you were at school, you most probably lied to your parents. If one of them was a smoker, you probably stole cigarettes from them. I know if I ever found that my father had left his cigarettes lying around, the challenge was how many I could take without making him suspicious.
There are probably few smokers who have not lied to their doctor about how many cigarettes they smoke.

After I relapsed I could not bring myself to admit it, and I became a secret smoker. I gather this is a fairly common experience. Many people do not want everyone to know, and they try to hide the fact that they smoke. This is of course deceitful, and although you may not actually tell anybody a lie, it is for all practical purposes no different. The problem with this is that you inevitably get found out. You feel awfully ashamed and wish you could escape somehow, so you lie. You most probably play it down – "it was just this once" or "I only smoke about one or two a day."

For me the worst part was that I lied to those nearest and dearest to me and, like so many others, I lost their trust. It was no use my telling them that it was only my smoking that I was lying about. I could not help feeling that they were simply not sure. This made me feel like a real heel. Nothing I could do or say would convince them: I had lied, and they knew it, and they wondered how many other lies I had told them. So much of the life of a smoker is based on denial: of how many cigarettes we smoke, and how badly it has affected our health.

If you are lucky the guilt of your deceit will reach a point at which you can no longer tolerate it and you will be motivated to quit.

The self-deception
Smokers are generally aware of the fact that smoking is bad for their health. However, they often tend to hide from the truth. The doctor would tell me to quit and would assume that I knew exactly why he said this. The truth was that I actually had very little knowledge of the damage smoking was doing to me. I feared trying to find out because I felt the truth would

only increase my stress levels. The problem with this is that it is of no help to simply drive your stress levels up if at the end of it there is still no means of escape. However, this book will provide you with a number of ways of escape. An important first step in this is knowing all the details of what smoking is doing to you. Hiding from the truth will lead you further down the path of destruction than you want to go. You can find help if you will just look for it.

When ill, smokers tend to wait longer before visiting the doctor as they are scared of what he/she will say. If my wife knows I am going to the doctor, what if I have to tell her that the only cause of my cough is my smoking? I cannot tell you how many times I have been relieved when the doctor has prescribed medicine and I have been able to go home and tell my family that the doctor has diagnosed bronchitis. However, I still have to live with the guilt and the shame of knowing that in reality I would most probably not have got the infection if I had not been a smoker.

There is generally only a grudging willingness to admit that smoking has anything to do with our poor state of health, yet it is so often a contributory factor in things as simple as a common cold, sinusitis, asthma, or other illnesses such as bronchitis, coughing, poor circulation, and poor sexual performance. These are some of the illnesses that smokers regularly suffer from on their slow progressive path towards the more dreaded diseases such as heart attacks, strokes, emphysema, cancer and gangrene. Smokers tend to avoid reading articles or books dealing with the effects of smoking.

Many smokers hide from the truth until it's too late. We all think we will give up in time, but few manage to quit before they have done serious, permanent damage to their health. Please do not let that be you. Beware: there are many smokers who even following a heart attack have gone back to smoking. I was one of them. Don't let it get that sort of hold on you.

After quitting
If you speak to ex-smokers about life after smoking you will hear joyous reports of how much better they feel in so many ways. Fairly obviously, they will speak of how their health has improved. They generally just feel much better, sleep better, cough less, exercise better and are so much more full of life and energy and able to enjoy physical activities.

Perhaps more important is the way they start to feel about themselves. They may speak of their new-found freedom, of a life of joy and serenity, a life of courage, hope and renewed ambition. People start to tackle things that had gotten left behind in the smoky mists of the past and some return to pick up their studies and take up new, more rewarding careers. That can still be you.

You are a slave to nicotine.

Your health deteriorates progressively.

Your emotions may become a mixture of self-loathing, shame, anger, longing and despair.

You remain convinced that you will stop before it's too late.

You are a depraved addict, insanely pursuing nicotine as it progressively robs you of your quality of life.

Guilt causes your stress levels to increase.

You are on a downward spiral towards an early and possibly painful death.

You can escape the trap.

Hiding from the truth will lead you further down the path of destruction than you want to go.

You are on a slow progressive path towards the more dreaded diseases such as heart attacks, strokes, cancer and gangrene.

Ex-smokers may speak of their new-found freedom, of a life of joy and serenity, a life of courage, hope and renewed ambition.

Keep reading: there is good news up ahead.

4.2. Day-to-day living
Planning your activities

Smoking controls every aspect of your life. Consciously or subconsciously you plan everything you do in order to accommodate your smoking. Before you go anywhere you ensure you have enough cigarettes. If you are going somewhere smoking is not allowed, you plan when and where you will be able to have your last smoke and when and where you will be able to have your next smoke after that. If you have to endure a long flight, you are probably one of the first off the plane so that you can rush to the nearest smelly smoking room. You regularly have to excuse yourself from company so that you can go outside to smoke, and you seldom realise how bad you smell when you come back.

Smoking limits your activities

As your health deteriorates – almost imperceptibly, at first – you slowly start to find that your physical abilities are deteriorating. Your energy levels drop and you slowly become less and less active. You may well attribute this to growing older, and the ageing process certainly plays a role. However, once you have quit I am sure you will find that much of this slowdown has been due to the effects of smoking. Smoking may well have prevented you from taking up some physically demanding hobby that you may not even be aware of. It may even have influenced your studies or career choices.

You may find that you tend to avoid social functions at which you will not be able to smoke. You might decline an invitation to the movies or theatre. If you go to a restaurant, you may be inclined to avoid the main part of the restaurant where the best vibe is and find yourself relegated to the smoky enclosure reserved for those social outcasts – the nicotine addicts.

Smoking limits your achievements

Many smokers will tell you that with hindsight they realise that they set aside certain goals and dreams and settled for less. Smoking sapped their energy and enthusiasm for life. You will hear stories of people who have quit and taken up all sorts of new activities. For many people, quitting is the start of a whole new and more rewarding lifestyle.

Smoking can cause you to miss all sorts of opportunities and can alienate you socially. Many ex-smokers will tell you that they only really found their true potential after they quit smoking.

> **Smoking controls every aspect of your life.**
>
> **Smoking limits your activities.**
>
> **Smoking limits your achievements.**

4.3. Contents of tobacco smoke

Nicotine is one of the most addictive psychoactive drugs known to man, on a par with heroin and cocaine. Not only is it a powerfully addictive drug, but it is also a highly toxic chemical that has been used in insecticides. If you were to inject the nicotine from a pack of cigarettes directly into a vein, it would probably kill you. When you inhale tobacco smoke, the nicotine is rapidly distributed via the blood stream to every tissue in your body. The good news is that the nicotine in your body is eliminated within a couple of days of quitting. The bad news is that the tar hangs around for a long time.

Despite nicotine being the chemical that causes your addiction and despite the fact that it is highly poisonous, it is not the main cause of the health problems for which smoking is responsible. Cigarette smoke delivers many harmful chemicals into your body. Some of them act very quickly (in as little as a few minutes) to impair virtually all of you bodily functions, while others accumulate to cause more long-term effects. Cigarette smoke contains thousands of different chemicals. These include numerous different carcinogens (cancer causing chemicals) as well as many other harmful chemicals.

The carbon monoxide found in tobacco smoke is the same as the deadly poisonous gas found in car exhausts. Carbon monoxide forms a relatively stable (long lasting) complex with the haemoglobin in the blood. It therefore affects the ability of the red blood cells to carry life-giving oxygen. Even the relatively small amounts found in tobacco smoke are sufficient to significantly reduce the blood's ability to carry much needed oxygen to all the different organs of the body. It therefore compromises the function of all organs, and does so with immediate effect.

One of the most damaging things about cigarette smoke is the tar that accumulates in your lungs, slowly smothering them and reducing your lung's ability to absorb oxygen.

Nicotine is one of the most addictive psychoactive drugs known to man, on a par with heroin and cocaine.

Tobacco smoke delivers many harmful chemicals into your body.

It impairs virtually all of your bodily functions.

Tobacco smoke contains numerous different carcinogens (cancer causing chemicals).

Tobacco smoke affects the ability of the red blood cells to carry life-giving oxygen.

Tar that accumulates in your lungs slowly smothers them, reducing your lung's ability to absorb oxygen.

Your escape route lies up ahead. Keep walking.

4.4. Potentially fatal diseases

Tobacco is considered to be the single most prevalent cause of preventable death globally. Millions of people die annually from smoking-related causes. It is widely reported that approximately half of all smokers who do not manage to quit will ultimately die of smoking-related diseases. Your odds would be better if you were playing Russian roulette. Perhaps even worse, hundreds of thousands of non-smokers die every year as a result of inhaling the tobacco smoke of others. I am sure none of us want to think of ourselves as being responsible for the serious ill-health or even the death of others, but the truth is that we could very well be. Most often those who have been most severely impacted by our smoking are those nearest and dearest to us. It is no longer time to procrastinate: now is the time to quit.

Even if smoking does not kill you, it will shorten your life significantly. Smoking harms virtually all the organs in your body (even your skin). It will therefore most definitely compromise your health and your quality of life very significantly. You can expect to start suffering the illnesses normally associated with old age at a much younger age than non-smokers. The sooner you quit the better, as the damage only gets worse over time.

It is not surprising to learn that respiratory and lung diseases are among some of the most common problems associated with smoking. Tar, which contains numerous different chemicals, some of them carcinogenic (cancer causing), accumulates in your lungs. I strongly recommend that you spend half an hour or so examining some pictures on the internet to see what a smoker's lungs look like. When you see the blackened, tar-covered mess that passes for a set of lungs, you will wonder how anyone could survive such a condition. I thought my lungs probably weren't too bad until I saw these pictures. Let me warn you, some of them are horrific. But you can still escape.

Lung cancer, which is one of the most common forms of cancer world-wide, is mostly caused by smoking. If you smoke, your chances of dying of lung cancer are more than twelve times those of a non-smoker. Unfortunately, the news gets worse. The risk accumulates over time, so the more you smoke and the longer you smoke the greater become your chances of contracting lung cancer. And in addition to lung cancer, smoking is also linked to other forms of cancer. The carcinogens in tobacco smoke are absorbed in the blood and distributed throughout the body. Other forms of cancer linked to smoking include cancer of the oesophagus, mouth, throat, bladder, pancreas, kidney, stomach, and cervix as well as leukaemia.

In addition to lung cancer there are two other primary lung diseases that are common in smokers, which seem unavoidable when you see what smokers' lungs look like: chronic bronchitis and emphysema. Collectively these two diseases are referred to as Chronic Obstructive Pulmonary Disease (COPD). If you smoke, your chances of dying of either of these two diseases are several times higher than those of a non-smoker. These diseases are in fact relatively uncommon in non-smokers. Emphysema reduces the elasticity of your lungs and can make you fight for every breath. Patients can be bedridden for years and need oxygen to keep them alive. There is no way of reversing the disease and it gets progressively worse until you ultimately die, usually after a prolonged period of dreadful suffering. You really don't want to go along this route. With chronic bronchitis you develop a cough that worsens over the years. In both cases your lungs lose their ability to transfer oxygen to your blood stream, which is hardly surprising given that your lungs are thickly coated with tar.

If the lung diseases are not enough to frighten you off, then let us move on to the cardiovascular system. This is the system that distributes blood and oxygen around the body and consists of the heart, veins and arteries.

Various cardiovascular diseases including heart attacks and strokes are regarded as being one of the leading causes of death in western societies. If you smoke you are approximately twice as likely as a non-smoker to die from one or other cardiovascular disease. In addition to heart attacks and strokes you are also more likely to contract blood vessel diseases such as aortic aneurism and peripheral arterial disease. Peripheral arterial disease is also known by a number of other names such as hardening of the arteries, peripheral vascular disease, poor circulation and vascular disease. Peripheral arterial disease can lead to other problems including heart attacks, strokes and gangrene. In some cases it can necessitate the amputation of limbs.

A doctor friend of mine told me of a picture he had seen of a man who had had his legs amputated at the knees and his arms at the elbows. This man then had a special holder made so that he could still continue smoking. Please read on and make sure you find out how to escape before you end up in the same predicament.

In this section we have looked at a number of potentially fatal diseases: nine forms of cancer (there are probably more), chronic bronchitis, emphysema, heart attacks, strokes, and peripheral arterial disease. If you see how your chances of getting one of these dread diseases are heightened by smoking, you will realise that your chances of avoiding all of them in a lifetime are probably zero if you continue smoking. The chance that one of them will kill you is about 1 in 2.

> **Millions of people die annually from smoking-related causes.**
>
> **Even if smoking does not kill you, it will shorten your life significantly.**
>
> **Examine some pictures on the internet to see what a smoker's lungs look like.**
>
> **Lung cancer, which is one of the most common forms of cancer world-wide, is mostly caused by smoking.**
>
> **Two other primary lung diseases that are common in smokers are chronic bronchitis and emphysema.**
>
> **Smokers are approximately twice as likely as non-smokers to die from a cardiovascular disease.**
>
> **Peripheral arterial disease can lead to other problems, including heart attacks, strokes and gangrene.**
>
> **Read on and find out how to escape the nicotine trap.**

4.5.   Smoking and reproduction

Smoking affects your fertility levels, almost every aspect of the health of the baby in the womb, and the health of the child growing up. More importantly, it is not just the health of the baby that is compromised, it is the baby's very life itself, both in the womb and in early childhood, that is at risk.

The risk of miscarriage is several times higher in women who smoke than in non-smokers. Babies of women who smoke are most likely to have a lower birth weight and the chances of them being born prematurely or even being stillborn are higher. This lower birth weight is directly linked to the increased risk of stillbirth or of the baby dying soon after birth. These risks, even though not as severe, also apply to some extent to non-smokers who breathe a lot of second-hand, or environmental smoke.

Babies of women who smoke are more likely to die of Sudden Infant Death Syndrome (SIDS – or Cot Death).

We have seen that the oxygen supply in a smoker's blood is diminished and that the blood carries a number of toxic chemicals. This has an impact on the baby's development in the womb and on the baby's development in childhood. It can ultimately have a negative effect on the rest of the child's life. The baby of a smoker is likely to experience slower mental and physical development than the baby of a non-smoker.

> **Smoking affects almost every aspect of the health of the baby in the womb, and the health of the child growing up.**
>
> **The baby's very life itself, both in the womb and in early childhood, is at risk.**
>
> **Keep walking.**

4.6. Second-hand or environmental smoke

When a non-smoker inhales tobacco smoke, this is referred to as second-hand or environmental smoke. When I first read about second-hand smoke I thought it could not seriously be a significant issue. However, I soon found that virtually every study on the effects of tobacco smoke listed second-hand smoke as a very serious problem. At least tens, but more likely hundreds, of thousands of people die worldwide every year as a result of second-hand smoke. If you smoke in the house or car you could be having a very significant health impact on your entire family.

Second-hand smoke slows the growth of children's lungs, thereby making them more susceptible to various lung problems.

It is estimated that an adult living with a smoker is at least 20% more likely to develop lung cancer. Children are even more susceptible. However, the effect will lie dormant for many years and they will only develop cancer much later in life.

Second-hand smoke can trigger asthma attacks in children. It also significantly increases the number and severity of attacks in children who are asthmatic. I suffered from asthma as a child and I can assure it is not

something you would wish on your child. For one thing, it can severely
hamper all physical activity and can affect their sleep at night.

Children raised in a home in which they are exposed to second-hand
smoke suffer from more respiratory ailments such as colds, bronchitis and
pneumonia.

> **At least tens, but more likely hundreds, of thousands of people die worldwide every year as a result of second-hand smoke.**

4.7.   Non-fatal diseases

All of these diseases can be suffered by non-smokers; the point however is
that smoking increases your chances of suffering from them. It also brings
forward the age at which you begin to contract the diseases of old age.
You age quicker and die younger. Many of these are degenerate diseases
that get worse with time. The following are a few examples.

Smoking increases the likelihood of you contracting gum disease, which
can in turn lead to the loss of teeth. It reduces the amount of collagen
produced, leading to premature wrinkling of the skin. There is an increased
risk of macular degeneration, which is one of the most common age-
related causes of blindness. Cataracts, which cloud the lenses of the eyes,
are also more common in smokers.

Don't worry too much about all the bad news. We still have to get to the
good news section of this book: the how to section, the solution to your
problem.

CHAPTER 5 - PHYSICAL ASPECTS OF ADDICTION

The physical or chemical dependence to nicotine addiction can be dealt with easily by using one of the various medications available. There is therefore no need to fear any significant physical withdrawal symptoms. In fact, many smokers quit without any noticeable physical withdrawal effects. Virtually all quit programmes recommend using medication, and studies have shown that medication can double or even treble your chances of quitting successfully.

It would be well worth paying your doctor a visit, preferably a few weeks before you plan to quit. He/she can advise you on the best medication for you. For certain medications you will require a prescription and will need to start your medication programme a week or two before your quit date, which is why it is best to see your doctor well in advance. Other medications can be started on your quit date.

I would strongly recommend that you include some form of medication in your programme.

5.1.   A word of caution
Medication is not something to be treated casually. Incorrect use can lead to serious negative results. Overdoses of some of the most basic anti-smoking medication can be fatal.
If you use any of the over-the-counter medications make sure (as with all medicines) that you read the instructions carefully and adhere to them. They are there for your safety and to ensure that you get the best results out of their use.

5.2.   Different medications
Medication can be divided into three different categories according to the way they work:
- Varenicline (commonly known as Champix or Chantix);
- Bupropion (also known as Zyban or Wellbutrin)
- Nicotine replacement therapy (NRT), which comes in a number of different forms.

Varenicline (Champix or Chantix)
Varenicline is a relatively newly introduced medication developed specifically to assist people wishing to quit smoking. It requires a doctor's prescription and you will need to start taking it at least a week before you initiate your quit attempt.

It works by interfering with the nicotine receptors in the brain. It minimises the symptoms of nicotine withdrawal and lessons the enjoyment a person gets from smoking.

Research indicates that it more than doubles the chances of a successful quit attempt.

As with almost any medication, a number of side effects have been noted, which your doctor will no doubt discuss with you. This is a relatively new medication and as a result the amount of research that has been done into side effects is still limited. Some potential side effects you should possibly be aware of are depressed mood, thoughts of suicide and attempted suicide. I took this medication and despite the fact that I was already being treated for depression I had absolutely no adverse side effects.

Bupropion (Zyban or Wellbutrin)
Bupropion was originally developed for use as an anti-depressant. It was subsequently registered as an anti-smoking medication and has been in use for this purpose for some considerable time. It reduces the symptoms of nicotine withdrawal by acting on chemicals in the brain that are related to nicotine craving.

Bupropion requires a doctor's prescription and you should start taking it approximately two weeks before you quit.

People who have certain medical conditions should not take this medication; your doctor will be able to advise you if this applies to you.

Nicotine Replacement Therapy (NRT)

Nicotine replacement therapy aims to provide small doses of nicotine that enable a smoker to quit without suffering any of the physical withdrawal symptoms. You will need other programmes to help you deal with the mental and spiritual side of quitting. Studies have found that people using one or other quit technique dealing with the mental or spiritual aspects can approximately double their chances of success by adding NRT.

Generally, NRT should not be used if you are still smoking, as this only serves to increase you nicotine intake. If you use NRT while you are still smoking it could have an adverse effect. There is some research being undertaken to see whether NRT can be helpful in getting people to cut down. It is important to be sure that you are not overdosing on nicotine, as it can affect your blood circulation and your heart.

There are certain medical conditions under which NRT is not advised or for which special precautions need to be taken. It is therefore probably best to ask your doctor if you have special conditions such as cardiovascular conditions, pregnancy etc.

In most countries NRT comes in a number of different forms, including patches, chewing gum, lozenges, nasal spray and inhalers. A doctor's prescription may be necessary for certain forms of NRT.

Physical or chemical dependence can be treated using medication.

Therefore, there is no need to fear any significant physical withdrawal symptoms.

Medication can double or even treble your chances of quitting successfully.

Wow! Some good news at last.

CHAPTER 6 - MENTAL AND EMOTIONAL ASPECTS OF ADDICTION

Most traditional programmes propose a number of steps or stages. Many of these different programmes follow fairly similar steps. I have modified the traditional model slightly to include some of the latest findings and to highlight the aspect of a changed lifestyle or a new dawn rising.

Recently, Robert West, Professor of Health Psychology and Director of Tobacco Studies at University College London, has hypothesised a slightly different approach. His research showed that approximately half of all successful quit attempts were spur of the moment events without any pre-planning. This led him to hypothesise an alternative model to the stages of change approach. This new approach is based on "catastrophe theory," which proposes that "motivational tension" builds up in the smoker's mind. This is a tension between those things that motivate the smoker to continue smoking and those that motivate them to quit. This tension is probably fairly well balanced most of the time, but the tension builds up and can reach a point at which a small trigger is sufficient to effectively "flip a switch" that triggers a strong desire to quit.

Robert West proposes a quitting programme based on what he refers to as the "3Ts." The first T is creating "motivational tension." The second T is providing a trigger. Once a quit attempt has been triggered, then the third T (treatment) is required.

In this book I plan to help you to build the required "motivational tension" and then provide you with the necessary trigger and offer you a choice of treatments. Different triggers are probably needed for different people, so I plan to include a number of them. The triggers will never be identified as such, so you will come across them without necessarily recognising them. However, you will hopefully suddenly reach a point at which you decide that you have reached the end of the road as far as smoking is concerned and you will be committed to quitting. Much of the focus of a large part of this book is on the treatment that follows the commitment to quit.

> Approximately half of all successful quit attempts are spur of the moment events.
>
> Professor Robert West's theory proposes that "motivational tension" builds up in the smoker's mind.
>
> He proposes a programme designed to create "motivational tension," providing a trigger and then providing treatment. This book is designed to enable you to do just that.

6.1. Commitment

In order to succeed you need to be fully committed to your quit plan and programme. If you are fully committed, you have won a major and crucial part of the battle – as is in fact the case in any battle. A lack of commitment is often one of the reasons why many quit attempts fail.

It is a good idea to actively work at building and strengthening you commitment. The more time you spend doing this and the more ways you find to strengthen your commitment the better your chances of quitting successfully will be. There are a number of commonly recommended steps that you can take to reinforce your initial commitment.

Telling family, friends and colleagues about your intention gives an extra boost to your commitment, as you do not wish to have to face them when you fail to press through. You can ask them to keep you accountable.

Ask family and friends for support and encouragement.

Set a quit date and announce it to family friends and colleagues. This helps focus your mind on the project. You now have a definite date, and there is no going back. Make good use of the time before your quit date to prepare yourself, to reinforce your commitment, to build a glorious picture of where you are headed, and to consider carefully what the alternative might hold in store for you.

Prepare a programme and make sure you know how you are going to build up motivational tension. Know what medication you will be using and what mental and spiritual programmes you will follow. If you are going to use a support group, identify that group and get started.

Starting to take medication a week or two beforehand can be a strong motivation to push through.

Many people find that once they are irrevocably committed they experience a sense of relief, a sense of clarity as to where they are headed, and a sense of power to succeed.

There are a number of areas where commitment is required: you need to be committed to your desire to quit smoking, you need to be committed to your new identity as a non-smoker, and you need to be committed to your quitting programme.

Once you have quit you need to continually reinforce your commitment on an ongoing basis. This can be done in a number of ways.
As your life slowly but steadily improves, it is easy to forget where you have come from. Many people recommend that you keep a diary or journal of your progress and regularly refer back to what you have recorded. Reflecting on where you have come from in your journey to freedom serves as an encouragement and strengthens your resolve.

The first section of your journal should contain a list of the reasons why you want to quit. Think of as many reasons as you can and keep adding to this list. Regularly refer to this section and remind yourself of the reasons why you quit. Another section of your journal will list the new goals that you have set for yourself. Consider your progress towards your goal, to a healthier, more serene, more energetic and more motivated you. In doing this your commitment will strengthen over time, making it progressively easier to stay free.

> If you are fully committed, you have won a major and crucial part of the battle.
>
> There are a number ways in which you can reinforce your commitment.
>
> Many people find that once they are irrevocably committed they experience a sense of relief, a sense of clarity as to where they are headed, and a sense of power to succeed.
>
> Once you have quit you need to continually reinforce your commitment on an ongoing basis.

Removing the fear of quitting

You need to analyse your fear for what it really is. Allen Carr refers to it as a confidence trick. NicA teaches courage and hope.

Fear is widely recognised as the overwhelming factor that prevents smokers from attempting to quit. Unfortunately, from all the literature I have been able to study, it seems as though this subject has not really been researched to any significant degree. There appears to be little understanding of exactly what it is that smokers fear or what the cause or real nature of this fear is.

Every night you climb into bed glad to be able to have eight hours of peaceful sleep, and you have absolutely no fear of the eight hours of withdrawal that lie ahead of you. Yet when you get up in the morning you can barely go an hour before you need a cigarette. What is the difference between these two scenarios? Why not just go another eight hours? After all, the worst of the withdrawal is behind you.

The fear factor affects everyone differently, so what follows is something of a generalisation based on the experiences of many smokers. Some people have attempted to analyse this fear by breaking it down into specific component fears. The basic fear appears to be a fear that the stress of trying to quit will be just too much to bear. This fear of stress feeds on itself, building up further stress. A number of other or component fears that have been identified include:

- The fear of not succeeding and appearing to be a failure in the eyes of others.
- The fear that the craving will be more than you can bear.
- The fear of a prolonged period of increased stress before you can feel totally free of all craving.
- The fear that you will have to fight your craving for the rest of your life.
- The fear that life will never be the same again.

People who have conquered this fear and have quit successfully generally find that their fear was largely unfounded.

Let's consider each of these fears on their own.

The fear of stress
Millions of ex-smokers have quit with very little stress at all. We have all heard stories of people who, deciding on the spur of the moment, have thrown their cigarettes away and never smoked again, seemingly without ever suffering any of the dreadful symptoms we are led to believe go hand in hand with such events – even sixty a day smokers. This book will teach you how to achieve the same effect so that you can quit with minimal stress.

As we noted in the section on understanding stress, smoking does not alleviate stress, it increases it. However, when you first quit you can expect to go through a brief period of increased stress before it starts to drop off. The stress caused by the physical effects of the nicotine should have all but disappeared within a few days. The stress due to the mental effects of addiction will last longer. There seems to be no clear indication in the literature as to how long this can last. As far as I can tell, significant stress from this source can last for weeks or, in some people, even months. After that time you can remain potentially susceptible to occasional cravings for years to come. However, these are so few and far between and so mild as to be no problem provided you recognise that you must never touch another cigarette, not even for a few puffs. We will deal with this aspect in more detail in the section on staying free. You can also find more on how to deal with stress in the section dealing with understanding stress. You don't need to fear stress: you should be able to manage it fairly easily.

If you feel that the stress may be a significant stumbling block, speak to your doctor who may be able to prescribe some form of medication to assist you.

The fear of failure
You will achieve that which you focus on. Let's focus on success – after all, that is the reason why you are reading this book. You have set your heart on success and there is no reason why you should not succeed.

You find what you search for. If you ask yourself why it is that you cannot quit, your mind will search for the answer. The answer to that question will be of limited use to you. It was the wrong question to ask. A far more useful question would be to ask, "How can I quit?" Focus on the answer, not the problem.

However, we must be realistic and consider the what-ifs. In the event of failure, there are a few important things to remember.

Firstly, you can join an exclusive club with a membership estimated to be in excess of one billion people worldwide: these are the people who have quit smoking and then relapsed. Most of them have gone on to quit successfully at a later stage. Many members have relapsed more than once. As Mark Twain said, "Giving up smoking is the easiest thing in the world. I know because I've done it thousands of times." Another thing to note is that it is estimated that there are in excess of one billion smokers worldwide. It is difficult to find a smoker who has not had at least one unsuccessful attempt to quit. You are not alone. Their number most probably includes kings and princes, heads of state and people from all walks of life.

Some figures suggest that only 4%–7% of people who attempt to quit are successful on their first try. However, if you use the right tools in the right combination I believe you can be almost certain of success. Using medicine and some form of support can improve your success rate to 20%.

In my first two "successful" attempts I simply reached a trigger point and quit on the spur of the moment without any medication or support. I believe we have the means today to re-write the stats.

If you relapse, consider your previous attempt at quitting as training, as it has been for so many before you. Learn from your mistakes and go for it again. Do not brood on your failure. Failure is simply one of the stages you have to go through on your way to success.

The most important thing to remember is that, once you have quit, never take so much as one puff on a cigarette ever again. This is probably the single best piece of advice that I can give you in this book. It is a piece of advice that has been given out many billions of times, and that has been ignored just about as many times. Just one puff almost inevitably leads you down the road to addiction once more.

Nicotine will always catch you at your weakest. The three biggest traps leading back to addiction are considered to be times of stress, alcohol and being in the company of other smokers. These are times when you need to be especially on your guard. Better still, leave the scene. If it is stress that is making you crave a cigarette, remember that nicotine does not relieve stress in non-smokers. The only stress it can relieve is that it causes.

Do not fear failure but rather focus on the new, healthier, more energetic, less stressful, more serene and more rewarding life ahead of you.

The fear that the craving will be more than you can bear
Many ex-smokers report that the cravings were not nearly as bad as they were expecting. I suspect that the common notion of how difficult it is to quit has been greatly embellished by urban legend. What we commonly hear in such instances are the worst-case scenarios, undertaken without any of the help available today. Any smoker who has attempted to quit unsuccessfully is prone to exaggerate the degree of difficulty they experienced in order to justify their failure. Such stories get added to our store of worst-case scenarios.

If you make a thorough study of the different methods available today then I believe you should be able to develop a tailor-made quit programme that will ensure that your cravings diminish fairly quickly to a more tolerable level.

The fear of a prolonged period of increased stress

Another common fear is the fear of a prolonged period of increased stress before you can feel totally free of all craving. I believe this is another mistaken belief driven by urban legend. As mentioned before, you can expect a short period of increased stress before the stress that was caused by the nicotine starts to fade. Cravings generally diminish markedly within a matter of weeks or, at most, months. If you use an appropriate quitting programme, they could diminish even more quickly.

Within months your cravings should be few and far between, very mild and of short duration.

The fear that you will have to fight your craving for the rest of your life
The level of craving you can expect to experience after a few months is nothing to fear, and it should continue to diminish for the rest of your life. But never ever be fooled into believing that you can have just one puff.

The fear that life will never be the same again

Indeed, life never will be the same again: it will just get better and better as you slowly recover from all the negative effects nicotine has had on your life. There is nothing to fear, only something to be elated about. Keep that in mind. The benefits of quitting so far outweigh the negative aspects that you will never want to go back. Build a positive outlook as you plan your quitting programme.

> Fear is widely recognised as the overwhelming factor that prevents smokers from attempting to quit.
>
> Every night you climb into bed glad to be able to have eight hours of peaceful sleep, and you have absolutely no fear of the eight hours of withdrawal that lie ahead of you.
>
> Fear of quitting is largely unfounded.
>
> Smoking does not alleviate stress.
>
> You don't need to fear stress, you should be able to manage it fairly easily.
>
> Set your heart steadfastly on success and set aside the possibility of failure.
>
> You only fail when you stop trying – try again.
>
> Failure is simply one of the stages you have to go through on your way to success.
>
> The three biggest traps leading back to addiction are times of stress, alcohol, and being in the company of other smokers.
>
> Cravings are usually less intense than expected, and even less if you follow the advice of this book.

6.2. The alternative to fear

If you know how, it can be much easier to quit smoking than is generally believed, and the basis for your fears is far less substantial than what you may have thought. NicA advises newcomers who fear not being able to quit to simply start tackling the process and in time they will reach a point when they are ready to quit. You can start planning a quit programme and start compiling a diary. Regarding their programme, they say, "It works if you work it." A lot depends on you having a positive attitude.

Some people find it helpful to follow the NicA philosophy of taking it one day at a time. Do not stress about the fact that you are going to have to do this for the rest of your life. Focus simply on today and it will get easier and easier with every passing day.

Build up a mental picture of all the really great benefits that will accrue to you. Focus on a new lifestyle rather than on giving something up. See it as gaining a new, more energetic, more serene and healthier life. As each day goes by, look at it as an accumulating achievement and praise God for the improvement in your health and all the other benefits.

Instead of focusing on your fears, focus on the things you will no longer have to fear. The threat of all those dread diseases will be diminishing – in some instances rather rapidly. You will no longer have to fear being trapped for hours on end in places where you cannot smoke. You will no longer need to fear the disapproving glances when you leave the room to find somewhere where you can grab a few quick puffs. Focus on all the improvements that you will be experiencing in your life. Focus on what you can do with the money you will be saving.

Being fully committed to quitting is a major help in overcoming your fear. This may be because you have changed your focus. Instead of focusing on what may go wrong, you are now focussing on what you need to do to ensure success.
If you have a time of prayer or meditation you can practice emptying your mind of your fears and replacing them with calm and peaceful thoughts.

One of my biggest problems with fear was that it prevented me from seriously seeking a way of escape. I would simply pray to God to help me with my addiction and leave it at that. It was not until I made a commitment to quit and then went down to the book store and purchased a book on the subject that I started to whittle away at my fears. By the time I had developed a programme and started taking a course of medicine to help with withdrawal, my fears had been largely allayed. I reached a point at which I looked forward to quit day with a mixture of excitement and apprehension, much like one would expect when setting out on some adventurous new project.

Simply start tackling the process and keep walking.
Stay positive.

Focus on a new lifestyle rather than on giving up.

Focus on the things you will no longer have to fear, like dread
diseases.

Keep reinforcing your commitment.

Look forward to your quit day as an exciting new adventure.

CHAPTER 7 - DEVISING A QUIT PROGRAMME

The better your quit plan, the better your chances of success.

7.1. Quit date

It is generally recommended that you set a quit date. This is important for a number of reasons.

It gives you the opportunity to do the necessary planning. It gives you time to build a clear picture of exactly why you want to quit. It gives you time to work on motivating yourself. It gives you time to build your commitment. It gives you time to plan a new lifestyle free of nicotine; time to plan your new dawn rising. It gives you time to decide what medication to use, and to start using it if necessary. It gives you time to identify the smoking triggers that could threaten to trip you up along the way and time to plan ways to cope with these triggers. It gives you time to ensure that when you finally reach the point of quitting you are thoroughly ready and have all the aids that you will need, ready and in place.

Some people like to pick a special date, such as New Year's Day. However, this is not generally recommended, as it is often difficult to implement a new discipline on celebration days. I chose a Saturday, which worked well for me: I could plan a routine that was different and I could undertake activities that kept me away from temptation. I got rid of all my cigarettes on the Friday night and when I woke up on the Saturday morning the first eight hours were already behind me.

7.2. Tell family and friends

This is very important. For me it was one of the most difficult steps, as I was a secret smoker. Originally I had smoked openly. After I quit the first time, I did not have the courage to openly acknowledge that I had relapsed into smoking again. For years I envisioned that if I ever had to quit again I would have to do it entirely on my own without any support and without anyone even knowing. Most people knew I was smoking, but it was something we did not talk about. Even if I managed to quit, I would not get any encouragement from anybody, partly because I would probably not tell anyone and partly because if I did tell them they would not know whether to believe me or not. For all they knew I may have just become more devious about my smoking

Eventually I hit one of those trigger moments. I realised I just had to quit, and that I needed support. I simply could not go down that road any longer: it was just too stressful in many different ways. I had to confess.

You need to call on family and friends for their support in this time. By telling them of your intention, you strengthen your resolve. A public declaration of your resolve raises your level of commitment and greatly improves your chances of success. You also establish communication links with people with a sympathetic ear who can support and encourage you in difficult times. When those nearest to you know what you are going through, they are more understanding of your struggle.

7.3.   Planning a quitting programme

Earlier it was mentioned that approximately half of all successful quit attempts were based on unplanned spur of the moment decisions. What then, you might ask, is the value of planning? To answer this I must rely primarily on my own experience. I have had two successful spur of the moment quitting experiences and one that was well planned over a period of some six weeks.

If you have already made a spur of the moment decision and are already into your quit programme, then you should most certainly continue. However, it is still worth learning as much as you can about quitting from the various books and literature available. This will definitely help to ease your path. Furthermore, much of what you learn you will still be able to use to speed up your progress towards the day when your occasional cravings are so few and far between, so weak, and of such short duration as to be of no concern.

Review the methods described in this book

As you study this book it will be worth taking special note of those suggestions that appeal most to you and considering how you can incorporate them into your programme. When I implemented my programme I found that I had incorporated a number of things that I either never used, or used to a minimal extent. The reason for this was that I just did not need them as the whole quitting process went much easier that what I had been expecting. When you select your programme, there is no harm in including more than you are likely to use. The important thing is to have enough in your programme to make it a success. When you come to implement the programme, you can just use what you feel is necessary.

Find out more about medication

It is a good idea to speak to a health care giver such as your pharmacist or doctor about the various medications available. There are various nicotine replacement products available in different forms, such as chewing gum, patches, nasal sprays etc. Most of these are available over the counter. However, it is most important that you are fully conversant with exactly how to use them if you are to get maximum benefit. Also, never leave nicotine gum lying around, as the nicotine it contains can be very poisonous in sufficiently largely doses. In addition to the nicotine replacement medications, there are a number of prescription medications that reportedly work very well.

Support services

You can consider using a support service. However, you need to recognise that we are all different. Some people find support services invaluable and have reported that they simply could not have ever quit without this support. Furthermore, they find them to be a great help in remaining free. To other people support services are of no use. I fall into this second category. If you think they may be able to help you, then you should definitely give them a try.

There are numerous support programmes available in different parts of the world. You can do an internet search for programmes in your areas. Organisations such as the United States Department of Health and Human Services National Cancer Institute, the American Cancer Society, the Centre for Disease Control and Prevention Department of Health and Human Services, and the Cancer Association of South Africa (CANSA) can generally be of help in this regard. Internationally, one of the best known support services is Nicotine Anonymous.

Set a quit date.

A public declaration of your resolve raises your level of commitment and greatly improves your chances of success.

It is important to have enough in your programme to make it a success.

Using medication can double your chances of success.

Consider using a support service.

CHAPTER 8 - PREPARATION PHASE

There are a number of different things you can do during your preparation phase that will make your quit attempt easier. These are discussed below.

8.1. Journal/diary

Possibly the best way to start is keeping a journal, which you will be using for a number of purposes throughout your quitting programme. It may be easiest to do this on a home computer if you have one. As you read the rest of this book, and especially the next few pages, you can start to make your own lists.

8.2. List how you feel and why you want to quit

Write a list in your journal of how you feel about your smoking. Write down some of the key points to keep on cards in your pocket. You need to do some serious soul searching and be completely honest. This list will serve a number of purposes: it will help you dig out feelings that you have possibly supressed for fear of having to face up to what smoking really means in your life; it will help to motivate you and give you the necessary conviction to quit successfully; it will be there as a constant reminder throughout your journey of what it is that you so desperately want to put behind you; it will serve as encouragement as your quitting programme progresses. Review this list and add to it regularly. The clearer the picture in your mind as to where you are headed, the easier it is going to be. Once you get started on your programme, you can periodically look back at your list and be grateful for how far you have come in your quest to be nicotine free.

Here are some questions and ideas that will perhaps help you with your soul searching:

- Do you worry about your health, and if so, what specific aspects?
- Do you find the many health warnings stressful?
- Which health warnings are the most pertinent to your life?
- Do you sometimes try and pass your cough off as a bout of flu or bronchitis when everyone knows it is due to your smoking?

- Do you find this and other similar situations embarrassing?
- Are you aware of the state of your cardiovascular system? Are you possibly heading towards a heart attack, stroke or arteriosclerosis?
- Does it frustrate you that smoking prevents you from doing many of the things you would otherwise like to do such as:

o things that require physical endurance?

o things that require you to be confined in a non-smoking area for protracted lengths of time?

o enjoying movies as much as you would if you did not have to stress about not being able to smoke?

- Enjoying long haul air, bus or rail travel.
- How do those near and dear to you feel about the state of your health? Do you really know, or is the subject taboo?
- Does the state of your health cause stress to others and, if so, does this concern you or do you simply put it out of your mind?
- Do you manage to do all the father/son, mother/daughter things you would like to do with your children, or are you just too old and tired and lacking in energy? Do you think it would make a difference if you did not smoke?
- Your family needs your support. Will you always be there for them? Will you be able to walk your daughter down the aisle or will you be confined to a wheelchair with a bottle of oxygen?
- Will you be a good grandparent to your grandchildren, or will you be too washed out to play much of a role in their lives?
- Do you manage your family responsibilities in a way that makes you proud?
- Have you added up how much money you spend on smoking every year? Is it enough for an annual holiday?
- Are there better things than cigarettes that you could spend your money on?
- Have you added up how much the additional medical costs resulting from your smoking have cost you?
- Have you realised that, as you get older, these costs will most likely soar as your body bears the pain of the affliction you have imposed on it?
- You could probably buy a nice car for the cost of heart bypass surgery.

- If you saved all the money you spent on smoking in a lifetime you would have enough to pay for several years of tertiary education.
- Do you feel bad about the things you could have done for your family with this money?
- Does your smoking make you feel guilty and ashamed?
- Does smoking disgust you? How do those near and dear to you feel?
- Do hotels always give you the second rate smelly rooms?
- How well do you manage at physical activities? Do you sometimes wish you could still play sport, or be more active in any way?
- How does your boss feel about the fact that you keep popping off for a smoke break?
- Would you want to employ someone who keeps popping out for a smoke and then returns to stress until the next smoke break?
- Do you think your smoking has possibly had a negative impact on your career in any way?
- Do you think you could perform better in your job if you did not smoke?
- Do you think you might have missed out on a promotion due to your smoking?
- Do you want to put all this behind you?
- What things would you do if it wasn't for the restrictions that smoking places on you?
- Do you find it tiresome/burdensome always to have to plan your activities in such a way that you can have adequate opportunity to smoke?
- Do you sometimes feel embarrassed in the company of non-smokers when you need to excuse yourself to go for a smoke?
- Do you often feel stressed because you have to wait before you can go for a smoke?

Once you have completed your list, write each one of these reasons on a card that you can carry in your pocket and refer to regularly.

Dig out feelings that you have possibly supressed for fear of facing reality.

What is it that you desperately want to put behind you?

Digging out these feelings will help to motivate you and give you the necessary conviction.

How do those near and dear to you feel about the state of your health?

Will you one day be confined to a wheelchair with a bottle of oxygen?

Do you manage your family responsibilities in a way that makes you proud?

Have you realised that, as you get older, your medical costs are likely to soar as your body succumbs to the affliction you have imposed on it?

Does your smoking make you feel guilty and ashamed?

Write each one of these reasons on a card that you can carry in your pocket.

8.3.   List the benefits of quitting

That was heavy stuff; now let's lighten up a bit. This is where you get to list all the positive benefits that will accrue to you once you have quit. Spend some time on this. You will need to do some soul searching here again. Nicotine use limits your possibilities, whereas quitting will enable you to develop a new empowering lifestyle and accept new challenges. The following list of questions and ideas will help you. Remember to make your own list of personal benefits in your journal.

Within as little as 20 minutes after you put out your last cigarette the health benefits start to accumulate. In addition to those diseases that have been directly linked to smoking, the health benefits of quitting relate to every aspect of your health. Your chances of contracting any illness are reduced, and your chances of a speedy recovery from any illness or disease are improved. These benefits can continue to accumulate for as much as 10 to 15 years. The following benefits, which are only some of those you stand to gain, are commonly quoted in much of the literature. Quitting benefits every aspect of your health.

- Within 20 minutes of quitting you are already beginning to benefit. Your heart rate and pulse rate both start to drop and your blood pressure starts to decrease.
- Within 8-12 hours the carbon monoxide level in your blood drops to normal levels and the amount of oxygen in your blood increases. This has a positive influence on every organ and system in your body.
- Within 2 days, your chance of having a heart attack has started to decrease. Your sense of smell and taste starts to improve.
- Within weeks, the decline in your lung function due to smoking has been halted. You have a reduced risk of asthma and respiratory infections.
- Soon after you have quit, the chances of smoking-related problems with pregnancy and the health of your unborn baby start to diminish.
- By the time you have reached 3 months, your chance of heart attack continues to drop still further. By this time your lung function and circulation have also started to improve.
- After approximately one month your coughing and shortness of breath starts to decrease. The tiny hair-like structures that move mucus out of the lungs start to function again. This increases your ability to get rid of mucus and clean your lungs. This in turn reduces your chances of contracting lung infections such as bronchitis and pneumonia. Your whole respiratory system will improve markedly over the next nine months or so.
- It is estimated that approximately one year after quitting, your risk of coronary heart disease will be half what it was when you were still a smoker.
- Ten years after quitting, your risk of lung cancer is about half of that of a smoker and your risk of other smoking-related cancers will also be significantly reduced.
- Over the period from 5 to 15 years after you have quit, your risk of

having a stroke can drop to the same level as a non-smoker. Similarly, after 15 years your risk of coronary heart disease has dropped to the level of someone who has never smoked.

- You will live a longer and healthier life than you would if you smoked.
- Your energy levels will improve. The improvement may be fairly slow, but if you could measure them you would see a marked improvement.
- Increased energy levels mean an increased quality of life.
- It is not just your physical health that will improve.
  It is common for ex-smokers to talk in glowing terms of new found emotional wellbeing and strength.
- Fears and doubts are commonly replaced by hope and courage.
- Your energy and zest for life will improve, and life will be more enjoyable.
- If you do get sick, you can expect to recover more quickly.

Other than just your physical health, your mental health and wellbeing will improve. The following are some of the typical emotions expressed by smokers regarding how they have felt after quitting.

- Your self-image and self-esteem improves as you no longer feel guilty and ashamed of being a smoker.
- You no longer have to hide from the truth regarding the dreadful effect that smoking is having on so many different aspects of your life, such as health, career, hobbies, physical activities, relationships, and mental health.
- You are able to do more things and feel good about them.
- You have a greater desire to achieve your goals.
- You have a more positive outlook on life.
- Your pride in who you are improves.
- You have more energy and focus.
- Your family life will improve in many ways as you no longer feel guilty about all the things your smoking is robbing your family of.
- You are able to engage in more open and warm relationships.

Wow! That is a long list of truly great benefits. I want you to think long and hard about all these benefits. Make your own personal list as it applies to you. You could put each of your personal benefits on a card that you can keep in your   pocket for regular reference. Ask yourself what you would be prepared to pay for these benefits and start thinking up a plan as to how you can get them.

> **It's time to change your lifestyle and accept new challenges.**
>
> **The chances of contracting any illness are reduced, and your chances of a speedy recovery are improved.**
>
> **Your whole respiratory system will improve markedly over the first year or so.**
>
> **After one year your risk of coronary heart disease will be half what it was when smoked, and still improving.**
>
> **You will start to enjoy increased energy levels and an increased quality of life.**
>
> **Ex-smokers talk in glowing terms of new found emotional wellbeing and strength, new energy and zest for life and improved self-esteem.**

8.4. Describe your new dawn rising

It is time to plan a new and empowering lifestyle that will strengthen your resolve to quit. What do you really want from life and how are you going to get it?

An important way to ensure that you are able to quit and remain free with the greatest degree of ease is to replace your smoking lifestyle with a new, healthier and exciting lifestyle. This means you will not simply be giving up something but, will be replacing your old lifestyle with a new one that is more interesting and rewarding. Do not focus so much on quitting as on the future. If you can build a glorious picture of a bright new future free of nicotine, and if you can focus on achieving this goal, it will be much easier to quit. Focus on where you want to go, not on what you fear.

Most other quit programmes that I have studied do not specifically speak about a changed lifestyle. However, most of them do actually recommend a change of lifestyle. This usually involves some form of exercise and/ or other physical activity, sport, hiking and possibly dieting. This is one possible lifestyle change. Many of them speak of taking up new hobbies or even new careers. Some people have gone back to studying. NicA recommends lifetime membership as a helpful lifestyle change. Once members have overcome the initial hurdles of quitting, they continue going to meetings and serve the organisation by helping newcomers to quit. In this way they give back to the community and this benefits them as it encourages and strengthens them to remain free. You can consider many other forms of community service. Christian programmes advocate that you change your idolatrous lifestyle of worshiping the god nicotine and start to worship the true God instead.

Changing your lifestyle can mean that every step along the quitting path has double benefits. Firstly, you benefit by becoming increasingly divorced from your addiction, and the strength of the hold it has on you diminishes every step of the way. The second benefit comes due to the fact that every step of the way brings you closer to achieving a new and rewarding lifestyle of your choice. This double benefit doubles your motivation and makes it easier to quit. As a result, the length of time before you feel completely free is diminished. Another way of looking at this is to consider that, as the neurological pathway that leads to smoking falls into greater and greater disuse, its prominence in your life diminishes, although it does not seem ever to actually disappear. At the same time, you are building a new pathway to support your new lifestyle that excludes smoking. This new pathway is becoming increasingly more prominent in your life day by day, overshadowing the old pathway.

If you have forgotten the dreams of your youth, now it is time to dream again. Consider all the wonderful things in life that smoking has robbed you of and ask yourself where you want to be in a year or two's time.

As you go about changing your lifestyle you may want to take it slowly. During the first few days you may only want to introduce one new aspect, such as walking. You may not be ready just yet for something possibly more disciplined, such as dieting. The idea is to slowly introduce more and more changes until you reach your goal.

> **What do you really want from life?**
>
> **Replace your smoking lifestyle with a new, more interesting and rewarding lifestyle.**
>
> **Focus on where you want to go, not on what you fear.**
>
> **Giving back to the community can benefit you.**
>
> **Changing your lifestyle means double benefits every step of the way and double the motivation.**
>
> **The neurological pathway that leads to smoking falls into greater and greater disuse.**

8.5.   Setting new values

Your values drive your lifestyle. Your new lifestyle needs to reflect your values, those things that are most important to you. You therefore need to consider carefully exactly what your real values are. Values can be categorised under certain headings. Here are a few to get you thinking. It is time to take out your journal again as you start to ask yourself what is really important to you. Sorry, but it is time to do some more work. Remember: quitting is easy, provided you work hard at it. The good news is that it's just hard work – nothing to fear, nothing to get stressed about. Keep walking.

There are different types of values. There are values you wish to strive towards and then, on the other hand, there are things you wish to avoid. You may value being loved and you may value avoiding poor health. There are ends values and means values. Exercise is a means value, which enables you to achieve the end value of health and physical fitness. You need to identify the end values you wish to strive for. Too many people are busy chasing money as an end value and have lost sight of their true end values. Money may be a means to acquiring a new car, and the new car may be a means of achieving a certain level of prestige.

Family values

Family values should probably be near the top of the list for most people. Solid, stable, loving families are the foundation on which solid, stable, loving communities are built. Research has shown that children from such homes do better in all walks of life than children who come from homes in which these characteristics have been undermined in one way or another.

Family values can include:

- Loving faithful husband and wife
- Loving and caring parents
- Stable family relationships
- Compassion
- A peaceful home
- Kindness
- Tolerance
- Endurance/perseverance
- Spending a lot of family time together
- Sharing family pastimes
- Disciplined and respectful children
- Parents setting a good example
- Physical, mental and spiritual health
- Balanced lifestyle

Decide on what family values you aspire to and write them down. Simply having a list and referring to that list regularly will reinforce these values. As these values become more central in your mind, so you will automatically behave in ways that are consistent with these values. If you wish, you can develop an action plan to implement these values in your life.

Family values can be undermined by smoking in a number of ways:

- Smoking can cause dis-harmony in the family
- Family members worry about the health of the smoker

- A smoker may by his/her actions be indirectly influencing his/her children to follow in his/her footsteps
- The smoker can waste a significant amount of the family budget (enough for an occasional holiday) on smoking
- Smoking robs you of energy, thus preventing you from participating as fully as you would like to in family affairs
- You may be too washed out to really do some of the things you would like to do with your children
- You may feel that you are less than what you should be to your family

Work values

Work values could include the following

- Honesty
- Integrity
- A solid work ethic
- Endurance/perseverance
- Tolerance
- Team spirit
- Being a valued member of your company
- Being a good example to others
- Progress in terms of promotion
- Being one of the best administrators/managers/etc. in the company
- Being popular/respected by colleagues and clients

Make a list of the work values you aspire to. Refer to this list regularly. You can develop a plan of action as to how you will achieve these.

Some ways in which work values can be undermined by smoking include the following:

- Smokers are continually going off for a smoke break and interrupting their train of thought. They then come back and spend the next hour or so getting increasingly stressed until their next smoke break
- Smokers have less energy than non-smokers and are able to achieve less

- Smokers are often less popular than non-smokers and not as well respected as non-smokers
- When it comes to promotion, smoking could subconsciously count against a candidate in the evaluator's mind
- Smokers could be less popular with clients

Health and vitality values

Health values can include:

- Physical health, including aspects such as medical health and wellbeing, physical fitness, weight control and a healthy immune system
- Mental health
- Spiritual health

Once again, make a list and a plan.

Physical health and vitality values can be undermined by smoking in a number of ways:

- As we have noted, smoking affects every organ and system of your body negatively
- It saps your energy and its negative effects are cumulative
- It causes you to age prematurely and ultimately robs you of your life years sooner than would otherwise be the case
- It lessens your self-image and causes stress
- It can cause a sense of guilt

The list of values goes on, including social values, religious values and so on. It is important for you to think about your personal values, because your values are important drivers in your life. A successful life is driven by a good value system.

> **Your values drive your lifestyle.**
>
> **Remember, quitting is easy, provided you work hard at it. It is just hard work – nothing to fear, nothing to get stressed about, so just keep walking.**
>
> **Exercise is a means value, which enables you to achieve the end value of health and physical fitness.**
>
> **Solid, stable, loving families are the fabric of which solid, stable, loving communities are built.**
>
> **Family, work, health and vitality, social, religious and other values can all be undermined by smoking.**

8.6.   New lifestyle

People who have quit typically find their new lifestyle most rewarding. Their newfound energy has enabled and encouraged them to become involved in all sorts of things. Some people have gone back to their studies and qualified for more rewarding careers. New energy levels enable people to get more done in a day, creating time to do things that would otherwise have been neglected. People have taken up things like music, sport, art, sculpture and writing.

This is a very important step. You don't want to make quitting simply a negative phase of your life that you have to get through. Adding a positive side to this experience by developing a new lifestyle should provide you with far more positive motivators than negative ones. This should make your adventure far more rewarding and it will be much easier to quit. This is your new dawn.

It is time to get out your journal again as you start walking through the list of things you wish to include in your new lifestyle. The following is a list to help get you thinking about some things you might consider including in your new lifestyle.

Healthy lifestyle (Get fit, get healthy, lose weight)
- Walking and jogging
- Gym
- Sport
- Diet
- Reduced food intake
- Healthy foods
- Food supplements
- Balanced life style
- Family time
- Exercise
- Relaxation
- Holidays
- Work
- Religion

Hobbies
- Art, sculpture, wood carving
- Pottery
- Music
- Different instruments
- Classical
- Band
- Military
- Boy Scouts / Girl Guides
- Hiking, rock climbing
- Sailing, boating, skiing
- Fishing
- Collecting
- Raising pets

8.7. Prepare strategies for your first few days

During the first few days you will most probably find that the urge to smoke is quite strong. However, the worst will soon be over and you will start to feel much better. Go easy on yourself for the first few days. Do not try to achieve too much: quitting requires patience. Generally, within three days

90% of the nicotine will have left your body. However, some people find that physical nicotine withdrawal symptoms may persist for a while longer as the body adapts to having no nicotine.

It is generally recommended that as you prepare for quit day, you prepare a strategy as to how you will deal with cravings as and when they come. There is a lot of advice to be had in the literature on this subject, and the following section is based on this advice together with my own personal experience.

For the first day of your quit programme you should plan a day of distractions that will divert your attention away from your normal routine that includes smoking. To achieve this, I set a Saturday as my quit day. This gave me two days in which I could find as many things as possible to distract me.

It is possibly best to start your quit programme first thing in the morning so that when you wake you already have eight hours of your new nicotine-free lifestyle behind you and you are well on your way on this first fresh new day of your new life.

Plan your day in a way that keeps you relaxed and happy, doing things that will keep your mind off smoking. For many people a good way to start such a day is getting some exercise by going to the gym or going for a long and relaxing walk. You do not need to do anything too strenuous. The idea is to get some exercise where you can breathe deeply and enjoy the fresh air as it starts to clean your lungs.

It is a good idea to try something new that you will enjoy. You might consider going for a cycle, going swimming or ten-pin bowling. Try going to places where smoking is not allowed, such as a mall, library, museum, art gallery, movie or restaurant. The more ways you can find to distract yourself the better. Remember that it is a good idea to plan in advance so that you have a long list of alternative things you can do, and then when the day comes, select what you want to do. It is once again time to start listing some ideas in your journal.

Try and stay away from things that might tempt you. Going to a friend's house for a barbeque and a few beers would be a bad idea. Alcohol usually heightens your desire to smoke, as does being in the company of other smokers.

If you plan to spend the day at home, you could possibly consider trying a new hobby, such as woodwork, painting, gardening, knitting or crochet. Do some spring cleaning or some home maintenance. Read a book, play solitaire.

During your first few days it is generally recommended that you try and avoid drinks containing caffeine. You should preferably drink lots of water or diluted fruit juice, as this will help to flush the nicotine and other toxins out of your body. As you drink, picture the liquid flushing the nicotine and the dozens of other toxic chemicals out of your body. You can drink up to eight glasses of water per day.

8.8. Identify triggers

Triggers are things that encourage you to light up. They can consist of various things, including:

- Visual signs, such as a pack of cigarettes
- Odours, such as the smell of tobacco smoke
- A cup of coffee
- Times of day, such as after a meal
- Having a barbeque with friends
- Certain places where you habitually smoke
- Activities, such as speaking on the phone
- Stress
- Alcohol
- Being in the company of other people who are smoking.

Triggers can also be feelings like anger, stress and disappointment. Some people see smoking as a way of coping with their problems, but in reality it just aggravates things. NicA speaks of four basic triggers: hunger, anger, loneliness and tiredness (H.A.L.T.). There are always other ways of dealing with these triggers.

For the next little while, every time you light up, think about why you did so. Make a list of these triggers so that you will recognise them for what they are once you have quit. You can then develop strategies for avoiding these triggers. Alternatively you can find different ways of responding to them. Triggers usually only operate for a brief moment or two, and once you have quit, their frequency soon diminishes markedly. There are many things you can do to distract yourself until the impact of the trigger has passed.

One of the most commonly recommended strategies is to do some deep breathing exercises when you feel tempted. Close your eyes, breathe in deeply and then concentrate on relaxing as you breathe out. Not only will this distract you, but it will also make you feel refreshed.

Commonly, people find something else to put in their mouths and chew on. This can be anything from gum, sweets, fruit, carrot sticks, nuts or even a toothpick. However, you should probably discontinue this practice after a few days, before it becomes some new undesirable habit.

You can get up from your desk and, instead of going for a smoke, you could go for a short walk, go and speak to someone briefly or go and make a cup of tea.
Relaxing and quietening your mind is a good strategy.

Make a list of things you can do instead of smoking, such as filing, washing your hands or washing dishes, or tidying a shelf in your cupboard.

During your preparation phase you need to try and identify as many of your triggers as possible and then devise strategies to counter these triggers whenever they arise. Especially in the first few days you should stay away from people, places and activities that might trigger a craving. If you cannot avoid smoking acquaintances, ask them not to smoke in your presence.

People who have quit typically find their new lifestyle most rewarding.

Don't make quitting simply a negative phase; add a positive side.

Developing a new lifestyle will add far more positive motivators than negative ones.

This is your new dawn.

Prepare strategies for your first few days.

Go easy on yourself.

Start first thing in the morning and plan a day of distractions to divert your thoughts from smoking.

After a good night's nicotine-free sleep you are off to a good start.

Get some fresh air and relaxed exercise.

Drink lots of water or dilute fruit juice to flush the toxins out of your system.

Avoid caffeine.

Be aware of triggers – avoid them or counter them with alternative actions.

Deep breathing, meditation or prayer and exercise are all good ways to avoid triggers

CHAPTER 9 - STARTING OUT

9.1. The night before

Most quit programmes recommend that, the evening before, you should get rid of everything that has anything to do with smoking. Get rid of all tobacco, matches, ashtrays, cigarette butts and anything that reminds you of smoking. Some people suggest that you wash your clothes and even the curtains so as to get rid of all tobacco smells. Another option would be to open all windows to let fresh air in and make liberal use of air fresheners. You could place a large poster that contains some positive message of encouragement on your bedroom door or other appropriate place ready to greet you first thing in the morning when you wake up.

9.2. The first few days

On your first morning, you should look on the bright side: today is the first day of a whole new more energetic and rewarding life. Do things differently today so that they can be a constant reminder of the bright future that awaits you.

Some people report finding that they felt grumpy or even angry for the first few days. Such feelings are fairly commonly associated with withdrawal symptoms. However, I believe they can be largely overcome by a change of attitude. Rather than saying, "Woe is me, I have this huge hurdle to get over," you should be saying, "I am so grateful that I have finally started on the path to a new, healthier, happier and more rewarding life and things are only going to get better from here on."

Remember that once you have those first few hours behind you, you never have to go back there again.

Avoid stressful situations and get lots of rest and a good night's sleep. When you are tired, your resistance drops and you are more susceptible to temptation.

Dealing with common hurdles
If you feel tempted, try and find something to distract you. You don't need to be distracted for more than a couple of minutes. Some programmes recommend what they refer to as the four Ds: deep breathing, discuss with a friend, delay, do something else.

Deep breathing is commonly recognised as a good way to relieve stress, anger, frustration and nicotine cravings. It almost seems as if there may be a link between things such as stress, anger, frustration and nicotine cravings. There are different ways to relieve nicotine cravings. I would generally stand up from my desk, close my eyes, and take a deep breath. Then, as I breathed out I would make a conscious effort to relax by dropping my shoulders. Another effective way is to raise your hands above your head as you breathe in and then drop them to your sides as you breathe out, consciously relaxing as you do so. It is also useful to concentrate on the fresh air entering your lungs and providing oxygen to your blood and subsequently to all parts of your body. Think of the healing that this is bringing to all the organs of your body. Another idea is to visualise a place that you can go to when you want to relax. You can then visualise this place whenever you do your deep breathing exercises and it will help you relax. Become aware of your breathing and slow it down. Do this for a few minutes.

Some people find that the distraction of chatting to a friend is a useful way of allaying a craving. If it is not an appropriate time to call, you could possibly send an sms.

Find something else to do. You do not have to be distracted for long before the craving will pass. Find something to chew on or go for a short walk, even if it is just down the passage to get something to drink.

The fourth D is delay. Interrupt your thought pattern. Count to a hundred and try think of something else. It may be a good idea while you are making lists in your diary to list some of the things you can think about when you are battling with a craving. It may be particularly helpful to think about different aspects of your planned new nicotine-free lifestyle. Think of the new things you will be doing. If you have time, you could delay by going for a walk or taking a bath.

As the days go by it is recommended that you record your progress in your journal. One reason that this is a good idea is that as you recover you can quickly forget just what it was like when you were still smoking. Having a diary helps you to measure your progress and this is a great help motivationally. Another reason is that, as you progress, you will from time to time think of new motivational ideas and it is useful to have a place where you can write these down and refer to them from time to time.

A change of routine can help. Try and think of the different things that trigger a desire to smoke. If you were in the habit of going outside for a cigarette after dinner, you might rather go and brush your teeth and then sit down to read a book. You need to try and avoid routines that involved smoking. If you were used to smoking while driving to work, try taking a different route and listening to a different radio programme. You will need to think about what you will do at the office in place of joining other smokers for a smoke break. Maybe you can find a non-smoking friend who does not mind helping out. Instead of joining the smokers, you could get a cup of tea and spend a few minutes chatting to your non-smoking friend. If you were in the habit of having a cigarette with a cup of coffee, you could try and drink juice or herbal tea instead.

Keep referring to your cards on which you have written down your reasons for quitting, benefits of quitting etc. From time to time it will be worth re-reading sections of this book or any other literature that you have found helpful.

Some people report that they have difficulty concentrating during the first few days of quitting. If this is the case, go easy on yourself: you will soon get your focus back.

Tense, restless feelings are common. It may be helpful to find something restful to do, such as trying your hand at some form of art, doing some gardening, arranging flowers or listening to music.

Dealing with anger
Some people find that, when they quit, their anger levels increase. However, this is usually a fairly short-lived experience. I believe that this is probably primarily a problem for people who naturally experience high anger levels. If you fall into this category, then it may benefit you to go on an anger management course before quitting.

Some of the things that help with stress relief can also help with anger. These include things such as deep breathing exercises and making a concentrated effort to relax.

> **It may be a good idea to start your quit programme first thing in the morning.**
>
> **The evening before, you should get rid of everything that has anything to do with smoking.**
>
> **Today is the first day of a whole new more energetic and rewarding life.**
>
> **Rather than saying, "Woe is me, I have this huge hurdle to get over," you should be saying, "I am so grateful that I have finally started on the path to a new, healthier, happier and more rewarding life."**
>
> **Avoid stressful situations.**
>
> **When you are tired your resistance drops and you are more susceptible to temptation.**
>
> **Remember the four Ds: deep breathing, discuss with a friend, delay, do something else.**
>
> **Concentrate on the fresh air entering your lungs and think of the healing that this is bringing to all the organs of your body.**
>
> **Having a diary helps you to measure your progress, and this is a great help motivationally.**
>
> **In your first few days try avoid routines that involved smoking.**
>
> **Keep referring to your cards.**
>
> **It may be helpful to find something restful to do.**

CHAPTER 10 - STAYING QUIT

Once you have quit, your memories of how badly smoking affected every aspect of your life will tend to fade and you will start to forget how badly you had wished you could just stop. Don't let your memories fade. Make sure you have a clear picture in your mind of just how bad it was. Write it down in your journal and keep referring back to it. Keep your motivation for staying quit just as strong as your motivation for quitting was in the first place.

Although it was important to understand the negative side of smoking in order to find the motivation to quit, it is more important to focus on the positive. Focus enthusiastically on your new lifestyle and note milestones along the way. I would go jogging in the mornings and slowly increase the distance I would jog. I also kept a close watch on my time. If you take up a new hobby or sport there will always be milestones you can aim for. Reaching these milestones gives you a sense of achievement and makes you proud of what you have put behind you.

Some programmes recommend that you reward yourself periodically. You can save the money you would normally spend on cigarettes and use it for this purpose.

How do you know when you can consider that your quit attempt has been successful? Different people define success differently. Some say that if you have been nicotine free for three months you can consider yourself to have quit successfully; others say it takes a year. I believe there are two main factors that determine your status with regard to how far you have come along the path to permanent freedom.

The first factor is the extent to which you have built a new reward pathway and weakened the old pathway. You will remember that we talked about the neurological reward pathway you had established in your mind that encouraged you to smoke. That pathway will slowly deteriorate with disuse and become progressively weaker. The more you build a negative picture of smoking in your mind, the more weakened this pathway will become.

At the same time, we recommended that you start a new lifestyle, and as you build this new lifestyle you will be establishing a new and ultimately a stronger pathway that precludes or discourages the smoking pathway. I believe the harder you work on your journal describing and reminding yourself of all the reasons you want to quit and the benefits that will accrue, the quicker the smoking reward pathway can be expected to be overruled by the new pathway. Keep referring to your journal. Make cards on which you list the main points and carry these in your pocket. The harder you work on your new lifestyle the quicker you will start to reap the benefits and the more you will be encouraged and disinclined to return to your old ways.

The second factor is that you need to convince yourself of the absolute rule that you can never have another puff. Although this is always a primary piece of advice that goes with all quit plans, most of us tend to think we are an exception to the rule. I know I did, and most smokers quit several times before they finally succeed, so I am sure many of them fall into the same trap. Where I used to believe that I could never ever risk just another puff, I now know that this is the case.
Just one puff stimulates your nervous system and wakens that giant reward pathway that is waiting for just such an event. It immediately gets greedy and wants more. Research has shown that if you have just one puff you are extremely likely to relapse completely.

The urge to smoke usually only lasts for a few minutes, so all you need to do is to find ways to distract yourself for those few minutes. You need to continuously be aware of the triggers that encourage you to smoke. As mentioned earlier, it is important to stay away from people, places and activities that might trigger a smoking response. Be ready to implement an avoidance strategy at all times. The triggers soon start to weaken and within a few months they should have disappeared almost completely.

All these diversions and new activities may distract you from your normal work and your productivity may drop. Don't stress: in a few days' time things will begin to pick up and soon you will probably be more productive than you have been in a very long time.

82

During your first few days it will be helpful to stay away from situations that could tempt you. Start thinking of yourself as a non-smoker and keep reminding yourself of all the benefits of your new lifestyle.

It is common to gain some weight when you quit smoking, so be on your guard. Reports suggest that gaining 5–10 kg is the norm. It seems to make no difference if you are already overweight: you will still only gain 5 – 10 kg. This is not unexpected, because food tastes and smells better once you have quit.
There are a number of things you can do to counter this.

One of the obvious things you can do is diet. Dieting is not easy. Someone trying to diet faces many similar challenges to someone who is trying to quit smoking. This is where the concept of a changed lifestyle can be important, as dieting could become part of this new lifestyle. It is a good idea to keep a record of your weight when you quit, as it will be one of your measures of success, particularly if you can keep it to just a few kilograms. When I first quit I did not have the motivation to contend with the stress of having to go on diet as well as that of quitting, and I picked up about 8 kilograms over a period of about three months before going on diet. Over the next seven or eight months I managed to lose this extra weight, but since then I have picked it up again. Statistics show that the weight you gain when you quit smoking tends unfortunately to be permanent.

The other obvious thing that you can do to control your weight is to start an exercise programme. As mentioned previously, the aim of such a programme is simply to get some healthy cardio-vascular exercise. You do not need to train as you would if you were planning to go out there and win races. Perhaps some 20 to 40 minutes, three or four times a week is all you need. If you want to increase the weight you lose in this way you could possibly exercise for a little longer and more frequently.

Another useful lifestyle change you can consider is to go on a detox programme. Make sure that this is a professionally designed programme and not just some fad diet.

One of the things many smokers fear most is the fact that staying quit is a long-term exercise. However, it need not be so. Within a relatively short period of time, the urge to smoke rapidly becomes weaker and less frequent, and you should be virtually free of cravings within a couple of months.

When they are finding the stress of remaining quit particularly difficult, many people find it helpful to call a quit-line. You can usually find one in your area on the internet or by asking your health care provider. You may want to look up their contact details during your preparation phase and write it down in your journal.

There are a few traps you need to be particularly wary of. These are among the most cited causes for people to start smoking again.

One such trap is times of emotional upset, such as feeling angry, stressed, worried, anxious or miserable. Despite the fact that it has been well established time and again that smoking only relieves the stress it causes, people still quote it as a reason for returning to smoking. Remember: that first cigarette may relieve some stress, but after that smoking will only serve to raise your stress level still higher.

Another common trap is parties, particularly where people are smoking and drinking. Drinking on its own can lower your resolve and can increase your risk of starting again. Simply being in the company of other people who are smoking can tempt you back to your old ways.

You need to recognise the difference between what is generally referred to as a slip and a relapse.

A slip is a one- time mistake that you can more easily recover from. A relapse is when you become a regular smoker once again. If you slip, it is time to be doubly on your guard. It is extremely easy to get hooked again. A slip requires immediate, firm and decisive action. Most slips lead to a relapse, although they need not do so.

Relapse starts with a slip. I remember the first time I relapsed. It was an evening when I was relaxing with a number of colleagues over a few drinks in a pub. A few of the guys were smoking and I decided to have a cigarette, thinking I would be able to quit again without any trouble. The next day came and went without incident, but the giant within had been wakened. It was not long before I thought that if I had managed to have one cigarette and then nothing for a few days it would not harm me to have one cigarette every few days. I went out and bought a pack. That pack only lasted a few days, at most.

It is best to totally avoid any slips, as they almost inevitably lead to a relapse. If you slip, it is best to quit again immediately after you have had only one or a few cigarettes. If you have relapsed and gone back to your old ways it may be better to set a new quit date and start again.

If you relapse it is vital not to get discouraged. Remember that failure is a common stage on the path to success. You can probably relax for a while and regroup your thoughts. Do not be too hard on yourself: pick yourself up and start again. Take this book out again and start compiling a new quit plan. Remember the things that worked the first time and try find one or two extra things that may help. Try and understand why you slipped. Find the trigger. Stay positive. Quitting is a learning process. Relapse can be deadly.

Make sure you keep a clear picture in your mind of the reasons you quit, and how bad things were before.

Try not to let this picture fade.

Focus enthusiastically on your new lifestyle and note milestones along the way.

The smoking neurological pathway will deteriorate with disuse, becoming progressively weaker.

As you build this new lifestyle you will establish a new, and ultimately stronger, pathway.

The harder you work on your new lifestyle the quicker you will start to reap the benefits.

Convince yourself of the absolute rule that you can never have another puff.

Be ready to implement an avoidance strategy at all times.

Consider ways to control the weight gain that almost inevitably accompanies quitting.

Within a relatively short period of time the urges to smoke rapidly become weaker and less frequent.

If you are finding the stress of remaining quit particularly difficult, call a quit-line.

Beware of the trap caused by times of emotional upset, such as feeling angry, stressed, worried, anxious or miserable.

Drinking and parties can lower your resolve and increase your risk of starting again.

It is best to totally avoid any slips as they almost inevitably lead to a relapse.

If you relapse, do not to get discouraged. Failure is a common stage on the path to success.

If you relapse, take this book out again and start compiling a new quit plan.

CHAPTER 11 - EXERCISE

Exercise is a great distraction from smoking. It lowers stress and reduces the cravings that make you want a cigarette. It burns calories and tones your muscles.

Exercise helps you recover from symptoms of smoking and can build feelings of achievement. Seeing that two of the organs that are most affected by smoking are your heart and your lungs, it would probably be best to focus on cardiovascular exercise such as walking, swimming and cycling. This type of exercise will help your heart and lungs to recover more quickly.

Nearly all quit programmes recommend exercise, and top of their list is usually walking. It is therefore recommended that you take up some form of physical exercise and that you get a specialist to advise you on what is best for you. In the absence of any specialist advice, the following are a few generally recommended guidelines.

Almost any form of exercise is better than no exercise. It is probably a good idea to choose some form of exercise that you enjoy and that you can therefore most easily motivate yourself to do. This could be walking, jogging, hiking, cycling, gym or some form of other sport.

Exercise programmes can be designed with different objectives in mind. Some are designed to get you fit for sport, others to improve your health. At this stage it is probably best to focus on a programme aimed at improving your health. Anthony Robbins defines fitness as "the physical ability to perform athletic activity, and health as the state where all systems of the body are working in an optimal way." Many programmes, like walking, concentrate on a limited number of aspects of health such as the cardiovascular system, weight and stress. However, when you first quit smoking such programmes are very beneficial in a number of important ways, and are hence often favoured.

It may be a good idea to schedule your first exercise activity for early on the first morning of your quit programme. This will allow you to start the day in a very positive manner. With the first eight hours of your quit programme behind you and some healthy exercise to get your system pumping the toxins out of your body you will feel exhilarated. This will in turn boost your motivation and help you to feel positive about the remainder of the day ahead of you.

Plan what form of exercise you are going to do in advance. If it is something you have not done before it may be a good idea to try it out a few times before your quit day.

Build up a mental picture of yourself exercising and imagine the good it is doing you. Look forward to starting your exercise programme. For the first few days exercise daily if possible, as this will be of great help to get through those first few days.

It can be difficult getting into a disciplined routine of exercising. However, once you have been exercising regularly for a short while and you have gotten into the routine, you will look forward to your exercise and will no longer want to be without it.

It is generally recommended that you start with a 5-minute warm-up period followed by a few minutes of stretch exercises. At one stage I used a heart rate monitor. On occasions when I neglected the warm-up phase I found that within about a minute or two after I started running my heart rate would suddenly shoot up to over 200 beats per minute. This helped to convince me of the importance of warming up. At the end of your exercise period you should slow down and cool off for a few minutes before you stop.

Depending on your state of health it may be advisable to get medical advice before starting any exercise programme.

All you probably need at the outset is some form of aerobic exercise that raises your heart beat, improves your health and cardiovascular performance and helps you control your weight. It is sometimes recommended that you raise your heart beat to approximately 75% of (220 beats per minute, minus your age). Another approximate formula is 180 beats per minute, minus your age. You should probably strive to exercise for 30 to 40 minutes a day for at least three or four days a week. If you cannot manage this, any exercise is better than nothing. A brisk walk will do. I use a combination of mainly walking interspersed with short periods (half a minute or so) of jogging in between.

Most forms of physical exercise will help you burn calories and control your weight, which is particularly important when you have just quit smoking. Your healthcare provider or your local gym can probably advise you on a suitable programme for your particular needs.

Simple daily changes in your routine can help to increase the amount of exercise you get: walking to the shops instead of taking the car, using the stairs instead of the lift.

Healthy eating patterns are always to be recommended along with healthy exercise.

Exercise is a great distraction from smoking.

Exercise lowers stress, reduces cravings, burns calories and tones your muscles.

Exercise helps you recover and builds feelings of achievement.

Nearly all quit programmes recommend exercise, and top of their list is usually walking.

Choose some form of exercise that you enjoy so that it is easy to motivate yourself.

Schedule your first exercise activity for early on the first morning of your quit programme.

Get your system pumping the toxins out of your body: you will feel exhilarated.

Look forward to starting your exercise programme.

Start with a 5-minute warm-up period followed by a few minutes of stretch exercises.

The exercise you need should be aimed at simply improving the state of your health.

Strive to exercise for 30 to 40 minutes a day for at least three or four days a week.

CHAPTER 12 - RELAPSES

Remember: having one or two cigarettes is considered to be a slip. If you slip, you should get back on track immediately, before your slip leads to a relapse where you return to your old ways. Relapses are unfortunately very common. However, it is much easier if you succeed the first time.

Although relapses are so common as to almost be a part of the process, they certainly do not need to be. With our current understanding of addictions, I believe you probably have enough tools to have a much higher chance of success the first time.

The most important thing about relapses is that you must not let a relapse dishearten you. Relapses should be seen as part of the learning curve. If you relapse, accept what has happened and do not waste time stressing about it. It is time to take out your journal and keep walking. Start re-reading the literature you used the first time and add some additional literature if necessary.

Start looking for the reasons that led to your relapse and write these down in your journal. Look for what the literature has to say about these situations. You can be sure that many people have fallen for the same thing as what tripped you up. The literature is bound to have some good advice as to what you can do next time.
Start developing a new programme. Be encouraged by the fact that you have joined the club of millions who have gone through the same experience. The difference this time is that you are much further down the track. You are now much nearer your goal.

The quitting methodologies described above are broad general methodologies whereby you can pick and choose bits and pieces as you like to make up your own programme. The three methodologies discussed in the next three chapters are relatively institutionalised methodologies that are often used as stand-alone methods. They are therefore each dealt with in their own chapter. Their teachings can also be used together with the methodologies described above. Having said that, Allen Carr advocates that you use his method exclusively, without adding any extras. Even using NRT is taboo in his eyes.

Relapses are unfortunately very common.

Although relapses are so common as to be almost part of the process, they certainly don't need to be.

Don't let a relapse dishearten you. See it as part of the learning curve.

If you relapse, take out your journal and keep walking. Start developing a new programme.

You are now much nearer your goal.

CHAPTER 13. ALLEN CARR

The late Allen Carr, a chain smoker for 33 years, tried unsuccessfully on many occasions to quit smoking. Finally, in 1983 he had what he describes as a "eureka moment" when the truth about smoking dawned on him. From that moment on he was able to quit smoking successfully. He subsequently wrote the book Easy Way to Stop Smoking, which has become an international best seller and which has been translated into more than twenty different languages. Allen Carr also established more than eighty quit smoking clinics in all parts of the world.

His method has certainly helped many millions of people quit smoking. You might well ask, if Carr's method is so successful, why would I propose any other? The reason is simple: Carr's method does not work for everyone. As mentioned earlier, everyone's smoking and quitting experience is different. I personally studied his book carefully and, although I found it very helpful, his methodology did not work for me. Many people find the help of a support group such as NicA invaluable, and some people say that they could never have quit without the help of such support. The whole idea of this book is to expose you to a number of different methods that have proven successful and then allow you to develop your own programme.

The Allen Carr method does not require will power; it's more about establishing the right mind-set. Having the right mind-set is an important aspect of most if not all quit programmes. It is about understanding the true nature of smoking and seeing it for what it really is.

In his book, Carr sets out to allay any fears smokers may have of quitting. He emphasises the fact that smoking has no real benefits – after all, it is one of the world's biggest killers. No one would willingly take up smoking if they knew where it would lead them. All it does is relieve the withdrawal symptoms created by the previous cigarette. The "relief" that you feel when you light a cigarette is simply due to the feeling of being "back to normal." This is the way non-smokers feel all the time. By lighting a cigarette you are trying to achieve a state that non-smokers experience all the time.

Unfortunately, every time you smoke you are also damaging your health in a cumulative manner.

He teaches that fear of withdrawal symptoms is the greatest hurdle preventing most smokers from quitting. Carr maintains that withdrawal symptoms are so small as to be almost unnoticeable. This method places great emphasis on removing this fear and showing that stopping smoking need not be nearly as traumatic as is commonly believed.

One way in which this method differs from most other methods is that it concentrates on removing the need or desire to smoke. Carr sees this as focusing on the real cause of the problem. Once you have removed the need or desire to smoke you are cured and you have become a non-smoker.Carr believes that once you have reached this state you will forever remain a happy non-smoker.

Carr likens nicotine addiction to a "little monster" that requires constant feeding. However, if you starve the little monster by quitting smoking, it dies within a few days. Regarding withdrawal, he says, "There's no physical pain, the misery that we suffer is that we are not allowed to have a cigarette. It's like having an itch that you aren't allowed to scratch."

He also describes the "Big Monster": the brainwashing we are subject to due to factors such as common beliefs, peer pressure, advertising etc. that encourage us to believe that smoking really is something we enjoy. He strives to show these false beliefs for what they really are. Possibly even more importantly, we are encouraged to believe that it really is difficult to quit. Carr states, "It's the brainwashing, the illusions, the confusion, the doubts, the uncertainty, the fears and the waiting for nothing to happen that causes the misery."

Allen Carr's method does not require will power; it's more about establishing the right mind-set.

The "relief" that you feel when you light a cigarette is simply due to the feeling of being "back to normal."

Carr claims that fear of withdrawal symptoms is the main thing preventing most smokers from quitting.

His method concentrates on removing the need or desire to smoke.

Once you have removed the need or desire to smoke, you are cured.

Carr likens nicotine addiction to a "little monster" that requires constant feeding.

Regarding withdrawal, he says, "There's no physical pain, the misery that we suffer is that we are not allowed to have a cigarette. It's like having an itch that you aren't allowed to scratch."

It's the brainwashing, the illusions, the confusion, the doubts, the uncertainty, the fears and the waiting for nothing to happen that causes the misery."

CHAPTER 14 -NICOTINE ANONYMOUS (NicA)

14.1. Introduction

NicA has been in existence for many years, and they have accumulated a wealth of knowledge based on personal experiences. Much of this knowledge is available in their various publications. However, there is a very wide variation between one person's experience and another's and therefore any specific piece of advice given may not necessarily be applicable to you. When the cap fits, wear it – otherwise leave it. The people who contributed to NicA's corporate body of knowledge are probably primarily people who find support groups an important tool in quitting. In this way their experience differs from that of many people.

This section cannot do justice to everything NicA can teach you and help you with, and it is therefore intended to provide a brief overview of some of the good suggestions that they recommend. It will also hopefully help you decide whether you wish to call on their help, or perhaps obtain some of their literature, some of which is available to read free of charge over the internet.

Having to recognise the NicA programme as a spiritual programme has been a problem for many people. However, many have found ways of overcoming this hurdle that are amenable with their beliefs.

There are a few things about NicA that should be noted. Firstly it is based very closely on the programme originally devised by Alcoholics Anonymous (AA) and uses a slightly adapted version of the same twelve steps. The second thing to recognise is that the AA programme was developed as a Christian programme. The Twelve Steps were originally one form of practical application of the basic Christian approach to overcoming sin. You must be very aware that, despite the fact that the Twelve Steps were closely based on Christianity, neither AA nor NicA are Christian programmes.

The NicA programme is referred to as a spiritual programme, rather than being linked to any specific religion. Its preamble states, "Nicotine

Anonymous is not allied with any sect, denomination, political entity, organization or institution." Each member is therefore free to believe in a higher power of his or her understanding. Many people find it difficult to accept having to place their belief in a higher power. This does not however preclude their joining NicA and benefitting from everything they have to offer. The NicA programme does not promise instant success. Rather, it is a process of attending meetings and doing your best to work the Twelve Steps. They also offer online support through internet and phone meetings. You are welcome to remain with the programme and in time you will reach a point at which you are ready to take the step of quitting. For some people NicA membership becomes a lifelong commitment that they enjoy. They often find such a commitment an important part of staying free.

An escalating series of negative consequences resulting from smoking is often what inspires a smoker to quit. The consequences of smoking are often in the form of a downhill slide resulting in deteriorating physical and mental health. For many this slide is arrested by some major health scare. For many, it is death.
Nicotine's negative effect on smokers' lives involves much more than just health effects. Life as a nicotine addict is most often based on denial.
If you examine your smoking habits carefully you are likely to find that nicotine rules your life in a number of ways. It can control when and where you take breaks, when and where you eat, who your friends are. It controls how you spend your free time. Whatever you do has to be planned around being able to get cigarettes and being able to have cigarette breaks.

NicA members have found that smoking can affect your choices and performance in many ways. It can negatively affect the way you spend your leisure time. It can cause you to miss many valuable opportunities. It can alienate you socially. It can make it difficult for you to concentrate when you are in the company of non-smokers and you need to get away for a smoke break. It is reported that people have turned down good job offers because the work environment was a non-smoking one. Smokers often believe that if they ever had a really serious illness they would quit, but in many cases this does not happen. Health warnings are generally ignored. People hide from the truth till it's too late.

After failed quit attempts, some smokers have become secret smokers rather than admit to family and friends that they have relapsed. Many even hide when they smoke and avoid the company of family and friends just to get the opportunity to smoke.

We have noted that unnecessary fear prevents most smokers from attempting to quit. Fear and anxiety about quitting often simply causes smokers to smoke more. If you fear that failure will lead to ridicule and shame, NicA recommends that you simply attend a meeting and get to know some of their members. Often, when people experience the mutual support of fellow addicts, this concern is eased. Some of their meetings are open meetings where you can go along with a friend who is not a smoker.

Smokers are usually full of good excuses as to why now is not a suitable time to quit. There will always be reasons why "now is not a good time"; don't let them destroy your future. NicA suggests that you should focus on the things that you can do now. If you do not feel ready to quit just yet, that is not a problem. It is not stopping you from attending NicA meetings.

Not being ready to quit is not stopping you from taking any one of many preparatory steps. It is not preventing you from reading this book and other literature on the subject. It is not stopping you from asking your healthcare provider about the different medication available. It's not stopping you from starting a journal and listing all the negative effects that smoking is having on your life. It is not stopping you from describing the new lifestyle you want to lead when you have quit. Having the right attitude is a major step in the process of quitting. Get yourself on the path and start walking. You have limited time to do this before smoking claims a price higher than you want to pay. Take one step at a time and you will come to the point at which you are ready to announce a quit date. Keep walking: the prize is up ahead.

NicA members have typically found that as they attend more meetings their attitudes gradually change. They learn that it is necessary to turn their will and lives over to a power greater than themselves. NicA reports that many people attending their meetings battle with the idea of having to admit that they are powerless and need to hand over to a higher power. However, in time many come to realise they have no other choice. Members learn humility and compassion. They gain more self-confidence, courage and hope.

Look for opportunities to make progress and take steps forward, practice one of the Twelve Steps, write something in your journal. At times even very small steps are what is needed, as they can get us going again after we have become stuck. Every step is a step of faith, and a step towards your final goal.

Some people use visualisations as a form of motivation. You can picture yourself throwing your pack of cigarettes away and feeling elated about it. You can picture yourself running up a flight of stairs without getting out of breath. You can visualise yourself lying in a hospital bed on oxygen as your last painful days draw to a close.
Do not minimise the truth or deny the risks, even if you are not quitting today. The truth may be awkward at first, but in time it can set you free.

Like most quit programmes, NicA suggests that you set a quit date. This gives you a definite goal to prepare for. It allows you to make a firm commitment. However, do not get stressed if it does not work out. Remember: you have only failed when you stop trying.

Once you have quit you should keep reading the literature you have available. As we have mentioned in other sections you can keep lists of the things that motivate you, such as the reasons you want to quit and the benefits that will accrue to you.

Keep a list of how things are improving: your energy levels, complexion, sense of taste and smell attitude, shortness of breath.

NicA sees nicotine addiction as a physical, mental, emotional and spiritual disease. They have found that anxiety and fear over the negative effects of nicotine may not be enough to motivate smokers to quit. Such emotions are more likely to encourage the smoker to continue in order to allay such fears.

NicA believes that there is no cure for a nicotine addiction and therefore, once you have quit, staying free becomes a journey that you pursue one day at a time. On a personal note, from my experience and that of those I have spoken to, the cravings most commonly virtually disappear within a relatively short period of time. However, from all accounts it seems that they never totally disappear, and just one puff many years after you have quit will most likely cause you to relapse and go back to where you started. I believe almost everyone finds it easy to remain free. However, it is just as easy to fall back into the trap and you will need to remain forever vigilant.

We have mentioned that it is helpful to design your quitting programme around the implementation of a new lifestyle. In this way you shift your primary focus away from the negative aspects of quitting to the positive aspects of enjoying a new lifestyle. NicA is about a new lifestyle of spirituality. People learn to change their lifestyle and find that their lives become more meaningful, fulfilling, joyful and productive.

The NicA programme is a spiritual programme.

The Twelve Steps of AA were originally a practical application of the basic Christian approach to overcoming sin. However, it is no longer a Christian programme.

Each member is free to believe in a Higher Power of his or her understanding.

The NicA programme is a process that takes time. You need to persevere.

Smoking often results in a downhill slide resulting in deteriorating physical and mental health.

Smoking can affect your choices and performance in many ways and can cause you to miss many valuable opportunities.

Unnecessary fear prevents most smokers from attempting to quit.

All you need to do is attend a NicA meeting and start working the Steps.

NicA recommends that you focus on the positive things that you can do now.

Members learn humility and compassion. They gain more self-confidence, courage and hope.

Some people use visualisations as a form of motivation.

Do not minimise the truth or deny the risks. The truth can set you free.

Keep a list of how things are improving, your energy levels, complexion, sense of taste and smell attitude, shortness of breath.

NicA members have found that anxiety and fear over the negative effects of nicotine may not motivate smokers to quit.

14.2. Twelve Steps of Nicotine Anonymous

NicA maintains that the Twelve Step programme "works if you work" it. NicA suggests that you practice implementing principles of the programme daily and work the Twelve Steps in order, ideally with a sponsor. A sponsor is a member who has experience working the steps, and is willing to offer individualized attention and support. Do not expect to be able to read the Twelve Steps and then to be able to go away and practice them effectively. NicA has found that people typically need to attend a number of meetings and to practice implementing the Twelve Steps for a while before they feel completely comfortable implementing them.

NicA Step 1
Step 1: We admitted that we were powerless over nicotine – that our lives had become unmanageable.

You need to recognise that you have lost control of your life and that you cannot solve the problem on your own. You need to accept your total lack of control over nicotine.

NicA Step 2
Step 2: Came to believe that a Power greater than ourselves could restore us to sanity.

If you are powerless to overcome your nicotine addiction then you need to look for a power outside of yourself, a power greater than yourself that you can draw on. If you can recognise this need, then you can start opening your mind up to new possibilities. You need to be flexible and willing. This is not a time for dogmatically clinging to unsubstantiated opinions, especially not if your life depends on it.

Some NicA members have found this concept difficult to accept. If you find yourself in the same position, I would strongly recommend that you do not write off NicA just yet, as they have helped countless people in your position. If you need a support group, they are certainly one of the best.

NicA Step 3
Step 3: Made a decision to turn our will and our lives over to the care of God, as we understood Him.

If you are still battling with the concept of God, don't give up just yet. NicA has been the way out for countless people like you.

During this step you may start to become more aware of your feelings and attitudes towards nicotine. You start to become more aware that you need help. You start to recognise that you need to humble yourself before a power greater than yourself if you are to receive the power you need.

You need to surrender and place your trust in your Higher Power.

NicA Step 4

Step 4: Made a searching and fearless moral inventory of ourselves.

During this step members are encouraged to list both their good qualities and the bad and to write them down. They draw on power from their Higher Power to be able to make a thorough assessment. This in-depth assessment helps you to plan a way out of the nicotine trap.

NicA Step 5

Step 5: Admitted to God, to ourselves, and to another human being the exact nature of our wrongs.

This is a step in preparation for change, humbly admitting that you have been wrong and repenting of your wrongdoing. It is a time to discard old negative thinking patterns and to introduce a new more positive way of looking at your future. It is a step of freeing yourself from your past.

This is the step in which you share the inventory you made in Step 5 with another person. Typically, you will choose someone who can be trusted and offer sympathetic understanding such as a NicA sponsor or another NicA member who has been down the same path.

NicA Step 6

Step 6: Were entirely ready to have God remove all these defects of character.

In this step you reaffirm that you are powerless to overcome you addiction on your own, you confirm your faith and surrender yourself to your Higher Power.

This is the point at which real change begins. You call on your Higher Power to remove your defects and to restore your health. You start to look at alternatives to your unhealthy lifestyle. This is your "new dawn," in NicA's case a new dawn of spirituality. You need to be willing to let go of past ineffective behaviours and attitudes.

It is important to recognise that what you are striving for is progress rather than perfection. Keep walking.

NicA Step 7
Step 7: Humbly asked Him to remove our shortcomings.

You need to have a proper perspective of yourself, which is why you need to become humble and ask for help from a Power greater than oneself, which some call "God." Being humble before God does not mean debasing yourself; it is understanding your place in the bigger picture of life.

It is a time to ask God to remove the stumbling blocks that are preventing you from quitting: the wrong perceptions, the fears, the uncertainties. It is time to detach yourself from your shortcomings and to look forward to a bright new future.

It is recommended that you regularly use prayer and affirmations to move yourself forward. Some NicA members use their Seventh Step Prayer as found in Nicotine Anonymous: The Book: "My Higher Power, I place myself in your hands and humbly ask that my character defects be lifted from me **so that I may help others**. Please grant me willingness, courage, and strength so that through my actions I may reflect your love and wisdom. Amen." Starting the day with such affirmations can get your day off to a good start.

NicA Step 8
Step 8: Made a list of persons we had harmed, and became willing to make amends to them all.

This step does not involve making amends. It is rather a time of preparation. It is a time to reflect on the harm that your smoking and other harmful or wrong behaviours have caused other people, places and things. It is time to make a list of people, places and things you have impacted and the manner in which you have harmed them and to become willing to make amends. It is not a time to try and justify your past actions but rather to humbly acknowledge your wrongdoings. Remember it is very often those nearest and dearest to you whom you have affected the most.

It is not a time to reflect on the wrongs that others might have done to you. It is a time purely to look at your side of the equation and ask what wrongs you have committed. It is time to prepare to clear away the damage caused by your actions and your actions alone.

NicA Step 9
Step 9: Made direct amends to such people wherever possible, except when to do so would injure them or others.

You need to approach those whom you believe you may have harmed and explain to them where you are in life. Explain that you have joined NicA and are making a concerted effort to put your smoking days behind you. Explain that as part of the programme you need to strive to put right the harm you caused others as far as this may be possible. You need to listen to their side of the story. Remember: it is not time to try and justify yourself, nor to remind others of any wrongs they may have done to you. Even if they should raise the wrongs they did toward you, do not pick up on this aspect. Listen and then leave it at that.

Many of us have given up numerous times so the person to whom you want to make amends may well be sceptical of your stated intent. All you can do is ask forgiveness and ensure that you do your utmost to stick to the programme. It can take time to re-build relationships, a time during which you need to demonstrate a consistent change of behaviour.

NicA Step 10
Step 10: Continued to take personal inventory, and when we were wrong, promptly admitted it.

You need to review your activities on a regular basis, ideally daily. Identify areas where you went wrong and look for ways that will help you avoid making the same mistake again. Consider also the things you got right.

NicA Step 11
Step 11: Sought through prayer and meditation to improve our conscious contact with God as we understood Him, praying only for knowledge of His will for us and the power to carry it out.

In all probability our relationship with God is not what we would ideally like it to be. Now is the time to change our lifestyle to one in which we seek God's guidance more earnestly. It is a time to build our relationship with God.

NicA Step 12
Step 12: Having the spiritual awakening as a result of these steps, we tried to carry this message to other nicotine users and to practice these principles in all our affairs.

NicA has found that it takes a lifetime of on-going effort to ensure that we remain free of nicotine use. The way in which they propose you do this is by suggesting NicA membership be a lifetime commitment. Obviously, you are free to leave the organisation at any time you wish. However, people find that by continuing to be a member and helping newcomers enables them to remain free. It keeps them practicing their new found life of spirituality.

As you begin to enjoy the experience of being free from nicotine there is a risk of thinking that you can control things, and having a cigarette just for fun. The best way to avoid this from happening is to share what you have learned from NicA with others. Helping others teaches you patience, tolerance and compassion. As you experience the joy of helping others, you grow spiritually and gain a new sense of your own worth.

Permission was granted by Nicotine Anonymous World Services to reprint the Nicotine Anonymous Twelve Steps above. This reprint does not imply Nicotine Anonymous affiliation with or endorsement of this publication.

NicA maintains that the Twelve Step programme works if you work it – i.e., if you keep walking.

People typically need to attend a number of meetings and to practice implementing the twelve steps for a while before they feel completely comfortable with them.

You need to look for a power outside of yourself, and greater than yourself, to draw on.

You can start opening your mind up to new possibilities.

You humble yourself before a power greater than yourself to receive the power you need.

You need to surrender and place your trust in your Higher Power.

Members are encouraged to write down both their good and bad qualities.

It is time to admit humbly that you have been wrong and to repent of your wrongdoing.

It is a time to discard old negative thinking patterns and to introduce a new, more positive way of looking at your future.

You call on your Higher Power to remove your defects and to restore your health.

You start to look at alternatives to your unhealthy lifestyle.

Ask God to remove the stumbling blocks from your path: the wrong perceptions, the fears, the uncertainties.

You need to approach those whom you believe you may have harmed and ask for forgiveness.

It is a time to build your relationship with God.

People find that continuing to be a member and helping newcomers helps them to remain free.

CHAPTER 15 - CHRISTIAN LIFESTYLE APPROACH - THE TRUTH WILL SET YOU FREE

This book is designed to provide you with sufficient guidance and motivation to enable you to quit, whether you accept the spiritual teachings or not. The Christian approach is a long-term approach that has the capacity to empower you to live a new life. However, Christianity does not provide any form of miraculous cure.

I want you to read this chapter with an open mind and see what you can learn from it. The Bible is by far the best substantiated book in the entire world library. It contains the truth that will set you free.

I also want you to remember that the Lord Jesus Christ made some of the most momentous statements in all of human history. If what He said was true, then no human on this planet can afford to ignore His statements.

One of the best known descriptions of who Jesus is found in the famous little book One Solitary Life by Dr James A. Francis (1864–1928). Francis wrote:

> "Here is a man who was born in an obscure village, child of a peasant woman. He grew up in another obscure village. He worked in a carpenter's shop until He was thirty, and then for three years was an itinerant preacher. He never wrote a book. He never held an office. He never owned a home. He never had a family. He never went to college. He never put his foot inside a big city. He never travelled two hundred miles from the place where he was born. He never did one of the things that usually accompany greatness. He had no credentials but himself. He had nothing to do with this world except the naked power of his divine manhood. While still a young man the tide of popular opinion turned against him. His friends ran away. One of them denied him. Another betrayed him. He was turned over to his enemies. He went through the mockery of a trial. He was nailed upon the cross between two thieves. His executioners gambled for the only piece of property he had while he was dying, and that was his coat. When he was dead,

he was taken down and laid in a borrowed grave through the pity of a friend. I am far within the mark when I say that all the armies that ever marched, and all the navies that were ever built, and all the parliaments that ever sat and all the kings that ever reigned, put together, have not affected the life of man upon the earth as powerfully as has this one solitary life."

Christianity contains bad news and good news. The bad news is all about us, while the good news is all about God. Let's begin with the bad news first. The Bible teaches that all humans are by their very nature born sinners, where sin is defined as an act that violates God's laws, that misses His mark of perfection. To sin is to err in our thoughts, words, and deeds.

The Bible tells us Adam and Eve sinned in the Garden of Eden and from that point on death entered the world, and from that day forward every human inherited Adam's sinful nature. This event, which took place in the Garden of Eden, is an important part of Christian, Jewish and Islamic teaching on sin (Surah 7, verses 19-25: The Glorious Qur'ân). The ultimate punishment for sin, any sin, is death. This death is firstly in the form of spiritual death or separation from God. The physical death we all suffer at the end of our lives is due to Adam's original sin.

You may well ask what this discussion about sin has got to do with a nicotine addiction? The simple answer is that smoking is sinful. That might sound rather harsh. After all, why should someone who is genetically predisposed to nicotine addiction be regarded as a sinner? Remember, we have established that we are all sinners. The fact that you smoke does not single you out for any special condemnation. All of us are guilty of numerous sins. If you read Galatians 5: 19-21 you will find that your sin is in the same category as jealousies, outbursts of wrath, envy and murder.

The important thing is that, as we begin to understand that smoking is one of countless different ways in which we sin and that we are all sinners, and to understand the nature of our sins, the Bible opens up ways for us to deal with them and to overcome them. Furthermore, if we are able to recognise our sin and ask God for forgiveness, then we are able to open up a path for God's grace and healing.

Jesus' purpose in coming to earth was partly to show us how to live in accordance with the Word of God and partly to present Himself as the perfect sacrifice and to pay the price for our sins. In Romans 3: 23-26 (NIV) the Apostle Paul tells us, "for all have sinned and fall short of the glory of God, and are justified freely by his grace through the redemption that came by Christ Jesus." God presented him as a sacrifice of atonement, through faith in his blood, He did this to demonstrate his justice, because in his forbearance he had left the sins committed beforehand unpunished – he did it to demonstrate his justice at the present time, so as to be just and the one who justifies those who have faith in Jesus."

An important point to note is the statement that "for all have sinned and fall short of the glory of God" means that none of us a perfect life and, as such, we are all sinners. As sinners we cannot meet God's standard of perfection. We all need forgiveness of sins. Smoking is one of the sins we need forgiveness for if we are to be healed.

Our sins mean that we are deserving of death or permanent separation from God. However, Jesus Christ, who was without sin, was put to death on the Cross in our place. He paid the price or penalty for our sins and if we believe in Him we can receive eternal life.

Although they are sinners, those who believe in Jesus also receive a long list of wonderful attributes as a free gift from God. Christians are, amongst other things, "redeemed from the market place of sin," "children of God," "citizens of heaven," "under God's grace," and much more. Contrary to some other quit methods, it is these positive attributes that will be the primary focus of the Christian approach to quitting.

The secular world generally considers nicotine addiction to be a disease. My understanding is that they use the word metaphorically, as addictions do not fit the normal definition of disease. Addictions are not a diagnosable illness that can be treated in the normal medical sense, using medicines or other physical intervention. Having said that, I must add that the physical side of addictions can be treated using medicines. However, the solution for the mental and spiritual aspects has to come from the patient themselves. The cure is an internal solution that comes from the mind.

111

If you consider only the disease metaphor of addiction you limit the approaches you can use to overcome your addiction. One of the greatest dangers of the disease metaphor is that you lay the blame for your condition outside of yourself. In this way you abdicate from your responsibility to deal with the problem yourself and close off a whole avenue of attack.

The next question you may be asking is where the Bible speaks about smoking, and of course the answer is "Nowhere." However, the Bible has a lot to say about closely related problems. Our primary guide to all addictions in the Bible is drunkenness or alcoholism. Many studies on addiction and addictive behaviour place all addictions together, as they are in their nature very closely related.

In Galatians 5: 16-21a (NIV) we find some very useful guidance: "So I say, live by the Spirit, and you will not gratify the desires of the sinful nature. For the sinful nature desires what is contrary to the Spirit, and the Spirit what is contrary to the sinful nature. They are in conflict with each other, so that you do not do what you want. But if you are led by the Spirit, you are not under the law. The acts of the sinful nature are obvious: sexual immorality, impurity and debauchery; idolatry and witchcraft; hatred, discord, jealousy, fits of rage, selfish ambition, dissentions, factions and envy; drunkenness, orgies, and the like."

There are many good reasons why God calls us to forsake our sins. The following verses from the book of Proverbs give an interesting picture of the pain and suffering that sin brings on the addict.

Proverbs 23: 29-35 (NIV):

"Who has woe? Who has sorrow?
Who has strife? Who has complaints?
Who has needless bruises?
Who has bloodshot eyes?
Those who linger over wine,
Who go to sample bowls of mixed wine.
Do not gaze at wine when it is red,
When it sparkles in the cup,

When it goes down smoothly!
In the end it bites like a snake
And poisons like a viper.
Your eyes will see strange sights
And your mind imagine confusing things.
You will be like one sleeping on the high seas,
lying on top of the rigging.
'They hit me,' you will say,
'But I am not hurt!
They beat me, but I don't feel like it!
When will I wake up
So that I can find another drink?'"

If you are familiar with the Ten Commandments you will recognise that they designate a wide range of different types of sins. The first two commandments, and especially the second, are of most interest to us in our discussion of addictions. These are found in Exodus 20: 3-5a (NIV): "You shall have no other Gods before me. You shall not make for yourself an idol in the form of anything in heaven above or on the earth beneath or in the waters below. You shall not bow down to them or worship them;" Nicotine or any other addiction is effectively considered to be idol worship or idolatry. An idol does not need to be some traditional form of statue; the Bible also recognises idols of the heart.

When we fall into any form of idol worship our idea is to make the idol provide us with some pleasurable benefits. It is the same when we start smoking. We believe that we can get some pleasure and then stop smoking before we become addicted. But that very rarely happens. We invariably end up enslaved to our idol just as the Bible warns.

So now you hopefully have an understanding of the spiritual side of addictions. Nicotine use is a sin in the form of idol worship. We worship an idol rather than the Lord Jesus Christ. We tarried too long at the foot of our idol and now we have become enslaved to our idol.

> All humans are by their very nature born sinners.
>
> You require forgiveness of sins if you are to inherit eternal life in heaven.
>
> It is only if you believe that the Lord Jesus Christ died for your sins, was buried, and rose again that you can receive forgiveness of sins.
>
> Smoking is a sin in the same category as drunkenness, jealousies, and murder.
>
> It is a sin that can be classified as idolatry (idol worship).
>
> The cure is not an external one, as one might get from an operation or medication, it is an internal solution.
>
> Understanding the spiritual nature of your addiction opens an additional avenue of attack

15.1. Getting started

If you are to seek God's help, the first thing He requires of you is to become a part of the team. To become a Christian is very simple: all you need to do is to believe that Jesus Christ died for your sins, was buried, and rose again. 1 Corinthians 15: 1-4 (NIV): "Now, brothers, I want to remind you of the gospel I preached to you, which you received and on which you have taken your stand. By this gospel you are saved, if you hold firmly to the word I preached to you. Otherwise, you have believed in vain. For what I received I passed on to you as of first importance; that Christ died for our sins according to the Scriptures, that he was buried, that he was raised on the third day according to the Scriptures," This is the first and absolutely essential step. This sounds straightforward, but it is a step that most people struggle with and may need the help of a Christian friend or a pastor.

In the Bible James tells us, (James 5: 16 (NIV)), "Therefore confess your sins to each other and pray for each other so that you may be healed." (emphasis added). Note that James places confession ahead of healing.

Step 5 of the NicA programme is similar. It states: "Admitted to God, to ourselves, and to another human being the exact nature of our wrongs".

It is important to recognise that if you have accepted the Lord Jesus Christ as your Saviour and you have confessed your sin to God, he will forgive you. You can put the burden of your guilt behind you and reach out for the freedom that is your reward.

15.2. Submission to God's will
Submission to God's will may at first seem to be one of the more difficult requirements, as most of us are not ready to hand over our lives to God. We are so used to being in total control, and may be fearful of what He may require of us. However, this is an important step, and one that is also recognised by other programmes. The Third Step of the NicA programme involves turning your will and your life over into God's care.

Jesus teaches us that without his help we cannot achieve anything of permanent spiritual value. In John 15: 5 (NIV) Jesus has this to say: "I am the vine; you are the branches. If a man remains in me and I in him, he will bear much fruit; apart from me you can do nothing."

It is worth remembering that you were created by God to serve Him. The greatest success that you can have in life depends on you handing your life over to God. Paul tells us, (Romans 12: 1-2 (NIV)), "Therefore, I urge you, bothers, in view of God's mercy, to offer your bodies as living sacrifices, holy and pleasing to God – this is your spiritual act of worship. Do not conform any longer to the pattern of this world, but be transformed by the renewing of your mind. Then you will be able to test and approve what God's will is – his good, pleasing and perfect will."

15.3. A new life in Christ
One theme that has been emphasised in this book is that what is needed is a new, more stimulating and rewarding lifestyle to replace the old. Nothing can be more rewarding than getting to know God's purpose for your life and living it out. If you want to be truly free of your addiction you need to be able to focus on something else. This should preferably

be something that precludes smoking or where smoking would be a noticeable disadvantage. Being a Christian most certainly does not preclude smoking – all Christians are sinners. However, when you become a Christian the Holy Spirit will most certainly start to convict you of your sin. Over time you will slowly become more aware of your different sins and you will develop a desire to overcome that sin. Becoming a Christian will give you a new focus, a new purpose, new priorities and new values.

15.4. Healing and growth

Healing and growth go hand in hand. As you grow as a Christian and get to know the Lord Jesus Christ better, so you are able to see life more the way He does. You begin to understand better what He can do for you, how He can strengthen you in your resolve, how He can motivate you, how He can protect you from temptation, how He can lead you. You gain a completely new perspective on life. You become a stronger and wiser person.

In 1 Corinthians 10: 13-14 (NIV), we find these very pertinent words: "No temptation has seized you except what is common to man. And God is faithful; he will not let you be tempted beyond what you can bear. But when you are tempted, he will also provide a way out so that you can stand up under it. Therefore, my dear friends, flee from idolatry." (emphasis added). These two verses worried me for a long time. I found it impossible to accept this promise and make it my own. I would pray to God asking Him to help me to give up. But somehow there was always an unspoken qualification: He had to make it easy, it had to be on my terms, not on His terms. God has never promised anyone an easy life, and it's always on His terms. In this life He offers you many challenges, and a chance to prove yourself and a chance to store up treasures in heaven. You need to consider the above verses carefully and pray to God that He will show you that way out. It is also a good idea to bear Paul's last three words in the above quote in mind: "flee from idolatry." As millions of smokers, alcoholics and other drug addicts learn every year, idolatry can be a truly deadly trap and they end up paying the ultimate price. Quitting may not be easy, but with God's help you can do it.

Some of the most important aspects of all quit programmes are things like perseverance, self-control and discipline. At first you may find that success eludes you; however, you need to persevere. Once you have quit, you will require a significant amount of self-control to maintain your quit programme before you can consider your efforts to be a success. Perseverance, self-control and discipline will need to become a part of your life from that point on. Fear of having to remain self-controlled and disciplined for the rest of your life is probably one of the main factors dissuading smokers from quitting.

We need to see what the Bible tells us about the qualities of perseverance, self-control and discipline and how it can be of assistance to us.

In Galatians 5: 22-23 (NIV), Paul tells us, "But the fruit of the Spirit is love, joy, peace, patience, kindness, goodness, faithfulness, gentleness and self-control. Against such things there is no law" (emphasis added). When you become a Christian you strive to become more and more like Jesus. As you study the Bible, spend time in prayer and become involved in church activities and fellowship with other Christians, so you grow in your Christian walk. Paul tells us that one of the natural consequences of this is that, as you grow, you can expect to start demonstrating the "fruits of the Spirit" more fully in your life. Thus your level of self-control is a characteristic that grows in stature as you grow as a Christian.

In 2 Timothy 1: 7 (NIV), Paul reminds Timothy, "For God did not give us a spirit of timidity, but a spirit of power, of love and of self-discipline" (emphasis added). You can expect to grow significantly in these powerful characteristics as you grow to be more like our Saviour, and they will enhance your ability to free yourself from nicotine.

Getting to know Jesus
How do we get to know Jesus? Fortunately, there are a number of ways.

As you spend time studying the Bible you get to understand Jesus' role in it from the very beginning. You will see the unveiling of the numerous prophesies foretelling His coming and describing what He would accomplish. When you read about His life, you will discover the most amazing person. His love, compassion, knowledge, His authority, His calm in control nature, just everything about Him is absolutely beyond compare. He was absolutely perfect in every way, a person no author could have

even begun to invent. The more you get to know Him, the more you stand
in awe and the more you desire to emulate Him.

As you spend time in prayer and consider your life through His eyes, and
as you meditate on the teachings of the Bible, so your understanding
grows and your appreciation of who He is grows.

As you grow to know Him you grow to admire Him more and more and you
desire more and more to emulate Him. In time your life's focus changes.
With all this you grow in the characteristics you need to quit smoking and
to remain quit.

Getting to know yourself
If you are an alcoholic, some of the secular programmes would
recommend that you should introduce yourself as "I am Jim, I am an
alcoholic," and they will tell you there is no cure for your condition. This is
neither a very positive outlook nor identity.

If you are an addict and you have accepted the Lord Jesus Christ as your
Saviour, then you are identified as a "redeemed sinner," "a child of God."
This offers a far more positive future.

God wants us to have a sober view of ourselves. He also wants to forgive
us our sins and have us put the past behind us and focus on the future
(a new dawn). Paul tells us, in Philippians 3: 12-14 (NIV), "Not that I have
already obtained all this, or have already been made perfect, but I press
on to take hold of that for which Christ Jesus took hold of me. Brothers,
I do not consider myself yet to have taken hold of it. But one thing I do:
Forgetting what is behind and straining toward what is ahead, I press on
toward the goal to win the prize for which God has called me heavenward
in Christ Jesus."

If we have believed in Jesus Christ, that He is the Son of God, God in
human flesh, that He was crucified to pay the debt we owe for our sins,
that He was dead and buried and that He rose from the dead on the third
day and that He now waits for us in heaven, then God wants us to put
aside that part of us that defines us as an addict. Instead, He wants us to
pick up the glorious future He has in mind for each one of us.

Conclusion

There is obviously an awful lot that can be said about the Christian approach to dealing with addictions, and in a book of this nature it is only possible to scratch the surface. You will need to get busy with your own study. Your local pastor can probably guide you in this regard.

Finally, remember that, whatever your quit programme, it is important to be fully committed.

Bibliography

Addictions and Recovery.org, *The Genetics of Addiction – Is Addiction a Disease?* (http://www. addictionandrecovery.org/is-addiction-a-disease.htm)

Agency for Healthcare Research and Quality: US Department of Health and Human Services, *Help for Smokers and Other Tobacco Users* (http://www.ahrq.gov/consumer/tobacco/helpsmokers.htm)

Allen Carr, Easy Way to Stop Smoking. Arcturus Publishing Limited, 2008.

American Cancer Society (ACS), *Guide to Quitting Smoking.*

American Cancer Society (ACS), Stay Away from Smoking (http://www. cancer.org/Healthy/ StayAwayfromTobacco/quitting-smoking-help-for-Cravings-and-Tough-Situations)

Anthony Robbins, *Awaken the Giant Within.* Simon and Schuster, 1991.

Cancer Association of South Africa (CANSA), *Kick Butt with CANSA.*

Centers for Disease Control and Prevention (CDC) (USA.gov), *Pathways to Freedom: Winning the Fight against Tobacco. Department of Health and Human Services.*

Centers for Disease Control and Prevention (CDC) (USA.gov), *Tobacco-related Mortality – Smoking and Tobacco Use.*

Centers for Disease Control and Prevention (CDC) (USA.gov), *Benefits of Quitting – Smoking and Tobacco Use.*

Centers for Disease Control and Prevention (CDC) (USA.gov), *Questions to Think About – Smoking and Tobacco Use.*

Centers for Disease Control and Prevention (CDC) (USA.gov), *Five Keys for Quitting Smoking – Smoking and Tobacco Use.*

Centers for Disease Control and Prevention (CDC) (USA.gov), *Health Effects of Cigarette Smoking – Smoking and Tobacco Use.*

Centers for Disease Control and Prevention (CDC) (USA.gov), *Quit Tips – Smoking and Tobacco Use.*

Centers for Disease Control and Prevention (CDC) (USA.gov), *Smoking Cessation – Smoking and Tobacco Use.*

Centers for Disease Control and Prevention (CDC) (USA.gov), *Winnable Battles – Tobacco Use.*

David Goldman, Gabor Oroszi and Francesca Ducci, *"The Genetics of Addictions: Uncovering the Genes."* Nature Reviews/Genetics, Volume 6, July 2005.

Earle Radmacher, Ron Allen & H. Wayne House, *Compact Bible Commentary.* Nelson's Compacttm Series, 2004.

Edward T. Welch, Addictions: *A Banquet in the Grave.* P&R Publishing, 2001.

Harvard Health Publications, *How Addiction Hijacks the Brain* (http://www.helpguide.org/ harvard/addiction_hijacks_brain.htm).

Helpguide.org, *How to Quit Smoking (*http://www.helpguide.org/mental/quit_smoking_ cessation.htm)

Helpguide.org, *Stress Management: How to Reduce, Prevent, and Cope with Stress.* (http://www.helpguide.org/mental/stress_management_relief_coping.htm)

Helpguide.org, *Understanding Stress: Symptoms, Signs, Causes, and Effects* (http://helpguide.org/ mental/stress_signs.htm)

Howstuffworks.com, *How Nicotine Works* (http://Science.howstuffworks. com/nicotine4.htm)

James Allen Francis, *One Solitary Life.*

Michael S Barry, *The Forgiveness Project.* Kregel Publications, 2010.

National Cancer Institute (NCI), *Clearing the Air.*

National Cancer Institute (NCI), *Harms of Smoking and Health Benefits of Quitting* (http://www.cancer.gov/cancertopics/factsheet/tobacco/cessation)

Nicotine Anonymous World Services Inc., *Nicotine Anonymous: The Book.* Fourth Edition. Author, 2011.

Nicotine Anonymous, Nicotine Anonymous: *The Programme and the Tools* (http://www.nicotine-anonymous.org/pubs_content.php?pub_id=499)

Neil T. Anderson and Mike Quarles, *Overcoming Addictive Behaviour.* Regal Books from Gospel Light, 2003.

Pfizer South Africa, *Stop Smoking Facts, Mytimetostart* (http://www.pfizer. co.za/RunTime/ POPContentRun.aspx?pageidref=2477)

Robert West, *"Catastrophic" Pathways to Smoking Cessation*: Findings from National Survey (http://www.nebi.nlm.nih.gov/pmc/articles/ PMC1382540/).

Robert West and Saul Shiffman, *Smoking Cessation.* Second Edition. Health Press, 2007.

Sciencedaily, *"Stress Contributes to Range of Chronic Diseases, Review Shows"* (http://.sciencedaily. com/releases/2007/10/071009164122.htm)

The Holy Bible: New International Version. Christian Art Publishers: International Bible Society – Africa.

No author, The Mindset of a Successful Quit Smoking Programme (http://quitsmoking. about.com/od/howto quitsmoking/a/mindsetstudy.htm)

The University of Utah, *Genetics is an Important Factor in Addiction* (http://learn.genetics. utah.edu/content/addiction/genetics/)

University of Maryland Medical Center, *Helpful Hints to Quit the Smoking Habit* (http://www.umm.edu/features/quitsmoking.htm)

US Department of Defence, *Stress and Nicotine: Which Comes First?* (http://www.ucanquit2.org/facts/StressAndNicotine.aspx)

US Department of Health and Human Services: National Institutes of Health: National Cancer Institute, *Clearing the Air: Quit Smoking Today.*

Wikipedia, *Aerobic Exercise* (http://en.wikipedia.org/wiki/Aerobic_exercise)

Wikipedia, *History of Alcoholics Anonymous* (http://en.wikipedia.org/wiki/History_of_Alcoholics_ Anonymous)

Wikipedia, *Health Effects of Tobacco* (http://en.wikipedia.org/wiki/Health_effects_of_tobacco)

Wikipedia, *Islamic Views on Sin* (http://en.org/wiki/Islamic_views_on_sin)

Wikipedia, *Jewish Views on Sin* (http://en.org/wiki/Jewish_views_on_sin)

Wikipedia, *Sin* (http://en.org/wiki/Sin)

Wikipedia, *Stress (Biology)* (http://en.wikipedia.org/wiki/Stress_(biology))

Wikipedia, *Twelve-Step Programme* (http://en.org/wiki/Twelve-Step_Program)

www.ingramcontent.com/pod-product-compliance
Lightning Source LLC
Chambersburg PA
CBHW070638030426
42337CB00020B/4066